91

Mistakes *Smart* Salespeople Make

HOW TO TURN ANY MISTAKE INTO A SUCCESSFUL SALE

TIM CONNOR, CSP

SOURCEBOOKS, INC.
NAPERVILLE, ILLINOIS

Copyright © 2006 by Tim Connor, CSP
Cover and internal design © 2006 by Sourcebooks, Inc.
Sourcebooks and the colophon are registered trademarks of Sourcebooks, Inc.

This publication is designed to provide accurate and authoritative information in regard to the subject matter covered. It is sold with the understanding that the publisher is not engaged in rendering legal, accounting, or other professional service. If legal advice or other expert assistance is required, the services of a competent professional person should be sought.—*From a Declaration of Principles Jointly Adopted by a Committee of the American Bar Association and a Committee of Publishers and Associations*

All brand names and product names used in this book are trademarks, registered trademarks, or trade names of their respective holders. Sourcebooks, Inc., is not associated with any product or vendor in this book.

Published by Sourcebooks, Inc.
P.O. Box 4410, Naperville, Illinois 60567-4410
(630) 961-3900
Fax: (630) 961-2168
www.sourcebooks.com

Library of Congress Cataloging-in-Publication Data

Connor, Tim, 1942-
  91 mistakes smart salespeople make : how to turn any mistake into a successful sale / Tim Connor.
      p. cm.
  Rev. ed. of: You call THAT selling : 91 dumb things salespeople do to sabotage their success.
  Includes index.
  ISBN-13: 978-1-4022-0812-6
  ISBN-10: 1-4022-0812-X
  1. Selling. I. Connor, Tim, 1942- You call THAT selling : 91 dumb things salespeople do to sabotage their success. II. Title. III. Title: Ninety-one mistakes smart salespeople make.

HF5438.25.C654 2006
658.85--dc22

                                                              2006021535

Printed and bound in the United States of America.
CH 10 9 8 7 6 5 4 3 2 1

BESTSELLING BOOKS BY TIM CONNOR

Soft Sell

The Voyage

Sales Mastery

O.K. God, What's Next?

Success Is a Choice

The Trade-Off

Above Ground

The Sales Handbook

How to Sell More In Less Time

The Ancient Scrolls

Life Questions

Crossroads—A Love Story

Peace of Mind

How to Be Happy AND Successful from A–Z

The Last Goodbye

Relationship Ruts and How to Avoid Them

52 Tips for Success, Wealth, and Happiness

Your First Year in Sales

That's Life!

Nit-pickers, Naggers & Tyrants

The Road to Happiness Is Full of Potholes

The Male Gift-Giving Survival Guide

CONTENTS

Foreword: Have You Met Seymour? vii

Introduction 1

Sales Quiz 3

Index of Mistakes 13

Index of Turn-Arounds 19

Chapter One: Attitude Mistakes 27

Chapter Two: Prospecting Mistakes 93

Chapter Three: Sales Presentation Mistakes 145

Chapter Four: Handling Objections and

                    Closing Mistakes 173

Chapter Five: Time and Territory

                    Management Mistakes 201

Chapter Six: Record-Keeping Mistakes 219

Chapter Seven: After-Sales Service Mistakes 231

Sales Quiz Answers 251

Personal Skill and Attitude Assessment 257

Summary 269

Afterword: Are Salespeople Becoming Obsolete? 273

Recommended Reading 277

Index 279

About the Author 287

HAVE YOU MET SEYMOUR?

Sooner or later every salesperson meets Seymour. Actually he spells his name S-E-E-M-O-R-E. Seemore needs to see more and more and more. He never buys, but he needs to see more.

Are you spending too much time with a Seemore? Do you have a lot of Seemores in your territory?

Seemores come in all shades, ages, sexes, colors, and sizes. They do have one thing in common, however: they never buy. They waste a lot of your time and corporate resources, but they never give you an order. And be thankful they don't. If they did, they would still want to see more throughout the relationship. One way to quickly identify a Seemore is his interest in brochures, demonstrations, references—just lots of stuff. In some cases, a genuine prospect will want to see some of this, but a Seemore wants everything.

So, what can you do with a Seemore once you have identified him?

One way to treat a Seemore, when you begin to feel you are dealing with one, is to ask him questions such as: In addition to all of this material I have provided you, what else will be necessary to get your business? When do you feel you will have enough information to make a buying decision? What is your decision process? What is your timing? You have to pin Seemore down.

And, once you've learned to identify Seemores, how can you avoid them in the future?

One way to avoid Seemores in the future is to be so busy and successful that you just don't have time for them. When they ask for lots of stuff initially, you can send it, but the next time they ask for more, come up with some reason not to accommodate them—corporate policy, you are on the road, literature is being reprinted, etc. Ask them if this additional information is critical for a decision and why.

Seemores are everywhere. They take your time and energy and generally create stress and frustration in your career. They often do a great job of convincing you that they are serious prospects. Don't buy it. Sometimes the best policy is to walk away from them if you can.

INTRODUCTION

There are only two ways to sell more. Do less wrong or do more right. Imagine the results you could achieve if you did both.

This book will help you avoid many of the costly deal-breaking mistakes that thousands of salespeople make every day. It will also give you techniques and strategies to ensure that you eliminate these mistakes from your sales behaviors and replace them with proven approaches that, when used with confidence, skill, and consistency, will help you break your sales records year after year.

91 Mistakes Smart Salespeople Make is not a sales manual. It is, however, a proven, straight-forward, no-holds-barred method for anyone in sales who wants to sell more in less time with less rejection and disappointment.

In my previous bestsellers *Soft Sell*, *Sales Mastery*, and *Your First Year in Sales*, I discuss a variety of concepts, principles, techniques, and attitudes that are required for success in selling. In this book, I cut to the chase to give you the essence of what makes selling work—one page for each common sales mistake most salespeople make and the formula for turning it around and making it work for you.

The 91 mistakes are grouped by major topic areas within the sales process. There are two ways to use or read this book: from beginning to end, learning and un-learning as you go; or going to the index and finding the specific mistake that you think you are making and referring to that page.

This is not a complicated process, but I highly recommend that you record your thoughts on each topic in the journal section at the end of the book. If you run out of room, you can always buy a journal for a few bucks. This journal section, over time, will become your most trusted resource for staying on top of the pile and avoiding sales slumps, disappointments, and lost sales.

SALES QUIZ

Write in or circle your answers before going any further (no peeking at the back of the book!).

1. One of the biggest mistakes salespeople make is…

_____

_____

2. Attitude is important in sales because…

_____

_____

3. Product features are…

_____

_____

4. Product customer benefits are…

_____

_____

5. The close of the sale is…

_____

_____

6. Sales objections are…

_____

_____

7. Three of the most important sales skills are…

_____

_____

8. The number one cause of failure in sales is…

_____

_____

9. Rank the following in order of importance as they relate to sales success:

___ Product knowledge   ___ Prospect qualifying

___ Sales skills   ___ Closing techniques

___ Attitude management   ___ Presentation skills

___ People skills

10. Why do people buy?

_____

_____

11. People buy emotionally/logically and then justify their decision emotionally/logically.

_____

_____

12. Your prospect will tell you ____ about how to get the sale.

_____

_____

13. Rank the following in terms of most prospects' concerns:

___ Price   ___ Good terms
___ Quality   ___ Organization reputation
___ Service   ___ Product/service reliability
___ Convenience

14. The close of the sale should start when…

_____

_____

15. People like to buy, but don't like…

_____

_____

16. What are your three best sources of new business?

_____

_____

17. The value of testimonials and references is…

_____

_____

18. You can sell something you don't believe in.
     ○ True   ○ False

19. When is the best time to ask a customer for a referral?

_____

_____

20. If you have a good product, it will sell itself.
    ○ True   ○ False

21. The objection you will have the greatest difficulty overcoming is…

    _____

    _____

22. You shouldn't ask for the order until you have covered all of the product features.
    ○ True   ○ False

23. Selling is an event, not a process.
    ○ True   ○ False

24. After-sales service can increase customer loyalty.
    ○ True   ○ False

25. It is harder to sell on the telephone than in a personal sales call.
    ○ True   ○ False

26. Verbal messages are more accurate than nonverbal signals.

        ○ True   ○ False

27. The most important element of the sales process is…

_____

_____

28. Once you have lost business, it is difficult to regain it.

        ○ True   ○ False

29. Every prospect deserves equal selling time.

        ○ True   ○ False

30. Cold calling is the least effective way to prospect.

        ○ True   ○ False

31. The Internet is making it easier to sell.

        ○ True   ○ False

32. The close of the sale is the end of the sales process.

        ○ True   ○ False

33. You can make up for a poor prospect with a good presentation and/or product.

○ True   ○ False

34. A planned presentation is more effective than a spontaneous customer-driven approach.

○ True   ○ False

35. It is better to ask more closed-ended questions than open-ended ones.

○ True   ○ False

36. If a prospect will see you, he/she is worth your time.

○ True   ○ False

37. You should make [number of] calls on a prospect until he/she buys.

38. People buy from people they…

_____

_____

39. Sales records are important because…

_____

_____

40. The number-one concern of most prospects is…

_____

_____

41. You can competitor-proof your relationship by…

_____

_____

42. If you are a good negotiator, you will close more
sales.

○ True   ○ False

43. A prospect profile is an effective way to prospect
because…

_____

_____

44. Solving after-sales problems is considered good customer service.

◯ True ◯ False

45. Should you plan your sales message in your office or in the prospect's office?

_____

_____

46. Every sales presentation should have a certain amount of small talk.

◯ True ◯ False

47. When a prospect challenges your price, you should…

_____

_____

48. Getting past the gatekeeper or voice mail is one of the most difficult challenges of a salesperson.

◯ True ◯ False

49. The two most important skills in selling are…

_____

_____

50. Anyone can learn to sell.
        ○ True   ○ False

*"The biggest human temptation
is to settle for too little."*

—THOMAS MERTON

INDEX OF MISTAKES

Attitude

1. Lacking Clear Focus
2. Stop Learning
3. Not Being Organized
4. Lacking Clear Purpose
5. Losing Your Excitement
6. Quitting Too Soon
7. Giving in to Self-Imposed Limitations
8. Seeing Failure as Negative
9. Trying to Do It All by Yourself
10. Lacking Gratitude
11. Being Pessimistic
12. Not Improving Your Self-Esteem
13. Not Believing in Yourself
14. Lacking Integrity

15. Getting Discouraged

16. Lacking Self-Discipline

17. Trying to Be Someone Else

18. Lacking Honest Intent

19. Letting Your Life Slip By

20. Being out of Balance

21. Lacking Patience

22. Letting Sales Slumps Get You Down

23. Lacking Clear Goals

24. Letting Your Ego Get in the Way

25. Not Managing Your Stress

26. Lacking Confidence in Yourself

27. Living Outside-In

28. Not Managing Expectations

29. Repeating the Same Mistakes

30. Seeing Problems as Negative

31. Living in the Past or Future

Prospecting

32. Selling Only by the Numbers

33. Selling at the Wrong Level

34. Being a Victim of Sales Cycles

35. Thinking People Buy from People They Like

36. Ignoring Past Clients

37. Staying in Your Comfort Zone

38. Letting Lost Business Go without a Fight

39. Not Routinely Networking

40. Asking, "Did You Get the Information I Sent?"

41. Being Afraid of Rejection

42. Not Practicing on Good Prospects

43. Talking Too Much

44. Losing Control of the Sales Process

45. Acting like You Need the Business

46. Not Building Trust Early

47. Not Asking Elevator Questions

48. Not Getting to the Decision-Maker

49. Not Knowing Your Competitors

50. Failing to Build Psychological Debt

51. Lacking a Precise Call-Back Approach

52. Not Asking for Referrals

53. Not Using a Prospect Profile

54. Not Becoming a Resource

Sales Presentation

55. Not Giving Tailored Presentations
56. Not Having a Concise Defining Statement
57. Selling Low Price Rather than High Value
58. Selling Features and Not Customer Benefits
59. Selling Everyone the Same
60. Not Relating to the Prospect
61. Seeing the Sale as a Transaction
62. Invalidating Prospects
63. Not Listening
64. Having a Poor Vocabulary
65. Failing to Create a Sense of Urgency

Objections and Closing

66. Not Disarming Objections Early
67. Seeing Price Objections as a Problem
68. Fearing Sales Objections
69. Projecting Your Personal Biases
70. Not Asking for the Business
71. Lacking a Closing Strategy
72. Advertising Concessions
73. Lacking a Lost-Sale Strategy

74. Lacking Walk-Away Power
75. Negotiating When You Should Be Selling

Time and Territory Management

76. Not Using Your Time Wisely
77. Using Technology as a Crutch
78. Losing Focus
79. Not Being Prepared to Sell
80. Poor Sales Forecasting
81. Poor Territory Management
82. Spending Too Much Time on Poor Prospects

Record Keeping

83. Not Keeping Records
84. Not Evaluating Your Results
85. Not Establishing Benchmarks
86. Failing to Improve Every Day

After-Sales Service

87. Lacking an Effective Follow-Up Process

88. Not Watching Trends

89. Not Asking

90. Going Only for the Home Runs

91. Not Seeing Current Customers as Prospects

INDEX OF TURN-AROUNDS

Attitudes

1. Focus on what you want, not what you don't want.
2. Invest 10 percent of your time and money in self-improvement.
3. Plan everything. Finish it. Then move on to the next thing.
4. Decide what is important in your life and never let it go.
5. Keep the passion alive in your career and life.
6. Never give up. Never. No matter how hard it gets.
7. You can do whatever you put your mind and energy to.
8. Fail often so you can succeed sooner.
9. Have mentors and a personal coach.

10. Feel and show gratitude for everything.
11. Be optimistic. You have nothing to lose.
12. Find ways to like yourself more every day.
13. Believe in yourself even when no one else does.
14. Always deal in the truth, no matter what.
15. Remember that all things pass. Just relax.
16. Remember, it is better to pay the price of discipline than regret.
17. Grow and change on your own terms, not those of others.
18. Do what you say you are going to do.
19. Start and keep a journal for your career success.
20. Live the balanced life you want to live.
21. Relax and enjoy the ride. Anything less could kill you.
22. Recognize that there will always be ups and downs in your career.
23. Spend routine time in goal-setting activities.
24. Keep your ego out of the sales process.
25. Recognize that your reaction to stress is entirely up to you.
26. Improve yourself every day.
27. Live inside-out.

28. Let go of illusions.
29. Learn from your mistakes.
30. Learn from adversity.
31. Stay focused in the present.

Prospecting

32. Prospecting is not about how many people you see, but about the quality of the prospect.
33. See effective selling not as a transaction, but as a process of building relationships.
34. Create a sense of buying urgency to control sales cycles.
35. Focus on establishing and building trust, not on being liked.
36. Stay in touch with previous customers.
37. Be willing to try new and creative approaches to prospecting.
38. Have a specific strategy for dealing with lost business.
39. Develop a regular routine for finding and meeting new people who can help you.
40. Develop an effective follow-up strategy and use it.

41. *Ask.* If you don't, you may never receive.

42. Practice new techniques on a fellow salesperson.

43. The prospect should be talking at least twice as much as you are.

44. Keep control with a planned approach.

45. Keep the focus on how the customer benefits.

46. Establish the prospect's trust before you begin to sell.

47. Develop several urgency-building, probing elevator questions.

48. Give presentations only to those who make buying decisions.

49. Learn everything about all of your competitors.

50. Create psychological debt through service.

51. Have an effective follow-up strategy.

52. Ask every customer and prospect for referrals.

53. Use a systematic method for qualifying prospects.

54. Be a business resource for all of your customers.

Sales Presentation

55. Tailor each presentation to the client's specific desires.

56. Know exactly what to say, regardless of the circumstances.

57. Create high perceived value so price is not an issue.

58. Ensure that prospects understand what is in it for them.

59. Customize your sales message and approach.

60. Always come from the prospect's perspective.

61. See the sale as part of an ongoing relationship.

62. Treat prospects with respect and concern.

63. Hang on the prospect's every word to ensure understanding.

64. Know the power of words and how they contribute to success.

65. Learn the prospect's dominant emotional buying motive.

Objections and Closing

66. Discover potential sales resistance early.

67. Never accept price as the primary objection.

68. Develop proven techniques for answering objections.

69. Stay neutral during the sales process.

70. Ask for the order.
71. Have a closing methodology that works and is repeatable.
72. Address concessions only when asked.
73. Know how to save lost sales before they are lost.
74. Know when a prospect is not a prospect and walk away.
75. Know when to sell and when to negotiate.

Time and Territory Management

76. Use your sales time wisely by planning everything.
77. Don't let technology replace the human touch.
78. Learn to compartmentalize your personal life and career.
79. Start. Act. Follow through.
80. Blend optimism with reality when forecasting.
81. See your territory as an abundant source of business.
82. Use a prospect profile to decide who is worthy of your time.

Record Keeping

83. Spend time every day writing down vital sales facts.
84. Evaluate your results weekly in order to plot better methods.
85. Create guidelines as standards to measure your success.
86. Spend time every day improving your skills and attitudes.

After-Sales Service

87. When in doubt, follow up.
88. Research trends that can impact your customers.
89. Learn to ask for what you deserve because of your service.
90. Establish the right mix of prospects in your pipeline.
91. Use your customers to help increase your contacts and sales.

CHAPTER 1

ATTITUDE MISTAKES

Attitudes. We all have them. Some contribute to your sales success while others sabotage your journey towards wealth, happiness, peace, and fulfillment. When was the last time you conducted a self-attitude audit? When was the last time you asked yourself, "How are my attitudes shaping my present and future?"

When was the last time you asked a customer, spouse, employee, supervisor, or friend how they feel about your attitudes? We shape our lives one day at a time, and we build our days one attitude at a time. Our destiny is nothing more than the daily accumulation of feelings and attitudes about ourselves, others, and our past, present, and future.

Guard your attitudes and remember that we tend to think and become like the people and things we are exposed to on a regular basis. Be careful of what you let into your inner world as well as who and what you let into your outer environment. Take a moment right now to assess the people in your life and their impact on your attitudes. Evaluate where you need to make changes in thoughts, perceptions, interpretations, and beliefs.

There is no right or wrong answer. The real question is: Are your attitudes helping you move more smoothly and successfully along the path of life?

In this first chapter we will cover many of the common attitude mistakes that sabotage salespeople's career success. My guess is that if you can avoid many or all of the ones listed here, you will be well on your way to setting sales records and achieving financial independence.

"Don't go around saying the world owes you a living. The world owes you nothing. It was here first."

—Mark Twain

MISTAKE #1: *Lacking Clear Focus*

You usually bring into your life whatever is consistent with your focus. You can focus either on what is not working or what is, what you don't have or what you do, what you want or what you don't want, what you believe in or what you don't. There is a great line that says, "Be careful what you ask for—you might just get it."

One of my favorite quotes is by the late tennis great Arthur Ashe. He said, "True greatness is, start where you are, use what you have, and do what you can."

Most sales winners are grateful for their blessings in life and focus on what they want, have, and can do. By the same token, most losers focus on what is missing, where they are not, and what they can't do.

Let me give you an example:

Salesperson A complains constantly. Prices are too high. Brochures are not up-to-date. He doesn't have a laptop or cellular phone. His territory is too small and has too few prospects. There is inadequate internal support staff. It's raining.... You get the picture. If this type of salesperson is doing poorly, he can find a reason why (other than himself).

On the other hand, Salesperson B—a winner—learns to work with what he has. He improvises, innovates, adjusts, compromises—whatever it takes to get the job done with the tools he has.

A key ingredient in all leaders, winners, effective people, and productive and successful organizations is focus.

Turn It Around

Focus on what you want, not what you don't want.

MISTAKE #2: *Stop Learning*

Is next year going to be better than last year, about the same, or worse?

Every year thousands of salespeople start the New Year with big goals, wonderful intentions, and executable plans. However, at the end of each year, thousands of salespeople can be heard asking themselves, "Where did I miss the boat? What did I miss? Why was this year not much better than last year?"

Over the years, one common denominator I have observed in successful salespeople is their willingness to invest in the continued improvement of their skills, attitudes, and philosophy.

What did you invest in yourself last year? Not in your bank balance, home improvements, travel, or daily maintenance, but in yourself. And you don't get to include what your company invested on your behalf in seminars, courses, or learning materials. If you are excelling in this demanding career, I will guarantee you have invested more in yourself than you have in going out to dinner. If you have invested more in personal entertainment, I will bet you are not achieving what you could be and that you end each month and year with frustration and worry.

Life is an interesting relationship between paying the price and winning the prize. Between self-investment and rewards. Between investing time in personal development and your ultimate success. It is never too late to begin an aggressive ongoing self-development program. There are hundreds of books to read, training CDs and tapes to listen to, and seminars to attend. Don't wait for your organization to invest in you and your future value. Take full responsibility for the quality of your life and learning. I strongly urge you to *do it now*.

Turn It Around
Invest 10 percent of your time and money in self-improvement.

MISTAKE #3: *Not Being Organized*

Clutter. Technology. Stuff. A full plate. Sales reports. Personal interests. Home life. Career. Relatives. Friends. Too little time. Too much to do. Meetings. The list goes on and on.

One of the things I have discovered about successful salespeople is their ability to handle a variety of tasks, problems, issues, responsibilities, and challenges at the same time. I am talking about personal management.

Below is a method for approaching personal management.

1. Start with a plan of what you want to do.
2. Prioritize your goals, objectives, tasks, projects, etc.
3. Stay focused.
4. Get rid of the clutter in your life.
5. Concentrate on one thing at a time.
6. Don't stick with anything that you are not passionate about.
7. Have routines for the regular tasks in your life.
8. Get up earlier. Go to bed later.

9. Organize your workspace so that you can be more productive.
10. Learn to say no more often.
11. Develop the habit of Doing It Now.
12. Don't make commitments you can't keep.
13. Respect and value your own time.
14. Play when it is time to play, and work when it is time to work.
15. Use technology as a tool, not a crutch.
16. Throw away the stuff you don't need, use, or want.

Turn It Around

Plan everything. Finish it. Then move on to the next thing.

MISTAKE #4: *Lacking Clear Purpose*

Loss of purpose in sales is akin to loss of faith in your ability to perform effectively and successfully. It is a feeling that no matter what you do, it will not be enough. It is those doubts and nagging questions that keep popping into your consciousness.

Purpose is the single most important motivator in a salesperson's life. It keeps you keeping on when everything around you is caving in—when nothing seems to work, when people have abandoned you, and when life seems to have forgotten that you exist.

There is no easy way to regain your purpose. It is a function of many elements: will, desire, resolve, faith, trust. Discovering or rediscovering your purpose takes time, effort, passion, patience, contemplation, self-evaluation, and commitment. These traits are not inborn or easily acquired, but in the end, once you own them, there is nothing that can stand in your way as you move into the rest of your sales career and life.

The first step in discovering your purpose is to find what you love, what you are passionate about, and why you are in a sales career in the first place. Most people live their lives always hoping for something better, but they either refuse or don't know how to do the work on themselves necessary to discover their purpose. I didn't discover mine until my late thirties after devouring dozens of sales and self-help books and contemplating hundreds of questions. Finally, it came to me, after more hours than I care to admit, in a laborious and often difficult self-appraisal: I want to help people with what I have learned on my life's journey. This led to my speaking and training career and, eventually, my writing as well.

Turn It Around

Decide what is important in your life and never let it go.

MISTAKE #5: *Losing Your Excitement*

Passion is the great equalizer. It can make up for a lack of experience and knowledge. I am not suggesting that you should not develop your knowledge or experience, however, because they will only enhance and further empower your passion—your strong belief in yourself, your mission, and your purpose.

Passion is different than enthusiasm. The cliché says, "Act enthusiastic and you will become enthusiastic." I have never subscribed to this philosophy. Why? Because if enthusiasm is an act that you use when things are going well, how do you behave when your life is falling apart? Are you just as enthusiastic about failure, about more problems than you deserve, and any number of disappointments, frustrations, and adversities?

Passion is not an act. It is a way of believing. It is woven into your cellular structure just as much as your DNA. Passion—real passion—for who you are, who you are becoming, where you are and where you are going, and what you believe in, stand for, and would die for shouts to the world, "I am here to stay, I am here to make a difference, I will leave my mark in this world. It may take me my entire life, but I will not give up until my purpose and destiny are realized."

Who do you know that is passionate about something? You can see it in their eyes, hear it in their voice, and sense it in their behavior. How are you doing? Are you in love with where you are, where you are going, who you are becoming, and what you are contributing? Or are you living like over 85 percent of the population with the attitude: "Same stuff, different day"?

If you have lost or are losing your passion for your sales career, do whatever is necessary to get it back.

Turn It Around
Keep the passion alive in your career and life.

MISTAKE #6: *Quitting Too Soon*

You would be amazed at how many people quit just before they are about to achieve the success they have been working toward. They just get tired of waiting, trying, or dreaming, and they give up. Why is this?

I believe it is for one of six reasons:

1. They really didn't want what they were going after in the first place.
2. They thought it would be easier.
3. They thought it would come sooner rather than later.
4. They lost belief in themselves or their mission or cause.
5. They let someone else discourage them or talk them out of wanting it.
6. They failed to realize that anything worthwhile takes time, faith, patience—and yes, action.

Is there an area in your life today where you are wavering? Thinking about giving up? I have been there. I know what it feels like to want to quit. But in the end, I realized I didn't really want to quit. I was just feeling sorry for myself. Not a pretty picture.

No one can determine another person's limits of endurance or courage. No one can judge what another person is willing or not willing to do. Never let anyone talk you out of your dream, no matter how well meaning they might appear.

Go for it. Keep at it. Just do it and enjoy the process. Don't expect that there will always be a crowd cheering you on. Much of success is enjoyed in quiet solitude, one moment at a time.

Turn It Around
Never give up. Never. No matter how hard it gets.

MISTAKE #7: *Giving in to Self-Imposed Limitations*

Smarter people than me have said, "The only limitations we encounter in life are those we place on ourselves." If this is true, why do so few people reach their full potential? Why do so many people feel stuck, out of control, and without hope in their lives? Why do so many people give up, quit, settle, resign themselves, or operate out of blame, anger, guilt, resentment, and self-pity when it comes to the quality of their life? If these questions were answered in a book, it would never sell. Why? Because the very people we are talking about here do not want to take responsibility for their lives. They insist on pointing their fingers toward something or someone else for the cause of their station or circumstances in life.

Each of us came into this world headed for greatness in some way. We were engineered for success at birth and conditioned for failure along the way. There is nothing we cannot do if we make up our minds to do it, then put our energy and passion into it.

At this point, the skeptics out there are thinking, *Sure, Tim, and I can fly.* I do not have the time or the interest to deal with skeptics or critics if that is their attitude. Certainly there are some physical limitations in some areas or with some people. My only point here is that most of us could do more if we would only learn that most of our ceilings are self-imposed.

What inner mental images are you holding in your consciousness that may be holding you back? Is it the fear of failure or success? Is it the fear of rejection or public scorn? Is it an inner feeling of unworthiness? Or is it some other emotional issue or scar that you have failed to recognize or deal with?

Turn It Around
You can do whatever you put your mind and energy to.

MISTAKE #8: *Seeing Failure as Negative*

If you are failing at something, great. You can learn more when things are going badly than when they are working. If you don't ever fail, you won't ever grow.

Is failure positive or negative? It depends. One person can experience a result, outcome, or consequence and give up, while another person can experience the same issue and use it to get stronger, wiser, or better in some way.

No one escapes this life without failures. I have had them. You have had them. Everyone has had them. The only way to avoid failure is to spend the rest of your life in some log cabin in the woods away from all human contact, expectations, and the need for achievement. I know of no one who has reached adulthood and has not had some form of adversity or failure in his life. Neither do you. Why then are we so afraid to fail? If I was worried or offended by those rejections from publishers who weren't interested in my book, I certainly would not be working on my sixtieth book right now.

So go out there and fail. Push. Try. You have nothing to lose and everything to gain. All success requires you to be tested on the anvils of time, adversity, problems, and life itself.

I know no one who has achieved great success and has not had his or her share of failures. Get in the habit of measuring your success, not by what you have achieved, but by how many times you have failed and come back again.

Turn It Around

Fail often so you can succeed sooner.

MISTAKE #9: *Trying to Do It All by Yourself*

There is a wonderful way to cut twenty years off the learning curve in your career: hang out with people who are where you want to be or people who have done what you want to do. The key is to create a win-win relationship. A mentor is one of many ways to accomplish this objective.

What is a mentor? A mentor is a person who is interested in your success, happiness, well-being, or future, and wants to make a contribution to it. These people don't necessarily have to be in the same business, have the same interests, or have been successful in their chosen field. What a mentor brings to the mentor/mentee relationship is insight, feedback, integrity, a willingness to help, and genuine concern for the mentee.

The mentor always gains something in this relationship, but it isn't always apparent what. You don't need hundreds of mentors. One can accelerate your career, two can skyrocket it, three can keep you learning and growing nonstop. I suggest you look through your contacts and see if you can find someone who can contribute to your career success and ask them to meet with you. If the person is a thousand miles away, just call them.

The key to a successful mentor/mentee relationship is setting the ground rules up front as to each person's role, expectations, agendas, time use, accountability, and feedback. The right mentors can save you time, energy, and money. They can challenge your thinking, hold you accountable, help you reach your goals, and help you have fun in the process.

Find someone who can help you. Take advantage of their insight, experience, and knowledge.

Turn It Around

Have mentors and a personal coach.

MISTAKE #10: *Lacking Gratitude*

Have you ever noticed that some people seem to have more of some things—or everything—than others? More fun, more stuff, more friends, success, money, influence, achievements, wisdom, peace, harmony, freedom...

Why is this? Over the years, I have observed hundreds of people in all walks of life, especially salespeople. As a speaker, I am privileged to meet thousands of people each year through my programs. One thing I have seen is a wide-ranging array of attitudes, feelings, and beliefs. It is interesting to note that the people I have met who have the greatest degree of peace, joy, harmony, life balance, friends, and success (however they choose to define it) are people who live with a great deal of gratitude in their lives.

Some of you might believe that you have nothing to be grateful for. Life is just "same stuff, different day," or just a bowl of pits, or not fair, or whatever. Here are a few things we have to be grateful for that many people take for granted:

1. Air to breathe and food to eat.
2. Bodies that work and minds that can think.
3. Books to read.
4. People who care about us.
5. Hearts that pump 2.5 million times a month.
6. Work that is satisfying, challenging, or contributes to our growth.

Refer to this list often. Refer to it when you feel sorry for yourself; when you have failed, been let down, lost your way; when you feel like quitting, feel good, feel bad; when you are sick, and when you are healthy. There is always a reason to be grateful.

Turn It Around
Feel and show gratitude for everything.

MISTAKE #11: *Being Pessimistic*

Is the glass half full or half empty? Will this product, policy, or strategy work or fail? Can I really achieve my dreams or am I living in fantasyland? These and hundreds of other questions are asked every day by well-meaning and hardworking salespeople.

In his great book *Optimism, the Biology of Hope*, written over forty years ago, Lionel Tiger discusses how optimism impacts a person's attitudes, outlook, success, and health. He suggests that people who are less optimistic about life, the present, and the future tend to get sick more frequently and often die sooner. In his book *Learned Optimism*, Martin Seligman discusses how each of us begins every project, activity, task, relationship, career, etc., with either a yes or a no—a yes, I can and I will, or no, I can't and I won't—in our heart.

You can't measure optimism. You can't bottle it, regulate it, run out of it, or manufacture it, but you can learn to develop it if you will only take the time and effort. Some people feel it is better to be realistic than optimistic—why set yourself up for disappointment? Tell me what is realistic. Looking back over the past one hundred years, where would we be if Edison, Bell, Gates, Ford, Land, and Disney had been realistic? If their attitude had been: "It hasn't been done yet, so I guess it can't be done"?

There are numerous benefits to having an optimistic outlook, and just as many pitfalls in not having one.

Here are a few of the benefits: you will achieve more, you will have more fun, you will be happier, you will have more friends, you will enjoy life more, and you will be healthier.

Turn It Around

Be optimistic. You have nothing to lose.

MISTAKE #12: *Not Improving Your Self-Esteem*

When you look in the mirror, listen to your own voice on a recording device, see yourself in a photo or on a video screen, is your first reaction:

- I could like myself better if...?
- I will like myself better when...?
- I'm really okay just the way I am?

When you fail, is your first reaction to:

- Blame others or circumstances?
- Take full responsibility for your own life outcomes?
- Begin again?
- Never try again?

When life gives you a problem, do you:

- Look for an excuse or scapegoat?
- Adjust?
- Quit?

When someone says unpleasant things about you, do you:
- Get angry at them?
- Accept their view as theirs and in no way related to who you are?

When you receive a compliment, do you:
- Make excuses?
- Say thank you?

When you succeed, do you:
- Pat yourself on the back?
- Belittle your success?

Turn It Around
Find ways to like yourself more every day.

MISTAKE #13: *Not Believing in Yourself*

Do you believe in, trust, and accept yourself? This is one of the keys to success and happiness.

Belief in yourself is the knowledge that no matter what crosses your path, you can handle it. No matter how hard you fall, how long you are down, or who is kicking you while you're down there, this too will pass and you can learn from the experience.

There are two types of people in the world: those who whine and those who act. Those who believe in a better tomorrow and those who don't. Those who blame and those who take responsibility. Those who resist the pull of life into the future and those who flow with it.

Self-belief says: "Throw it at me, life. I will handle it, overcome it, and I will survive and succeed."

A lack of self-belief says: "I quit. I can't do it. It's too much for me."

What is your approach to adversity, trouble, failure, problems, challenges, or any negative circumstances? Do you have a *yes* or *no* in your heart?

As you begin each new day, are you poised to *go for it*? To tackle whatever life throws in your path? To never give in or give up?

We won't do it *all*, have it *all*, learn it *all* in life. It just isn't that kind of world. But you have nothing to lose and a great deal to gain by pushing the edges and your limits. Trust the process of your life and the opportunities that cross your path and give it all you've got.

Turn It Around

Believe in yourself even when no one else does.

MISTAKE #14: *Lacking Integrity*

Integrity and trust go hand in hand as qualities for sales success. It is impossible to have one without the other. If you trust someone, it is most likely because they are trustworthy and they have solid ethics and integrity. If a person lacks either of the two, they generally will lack both.

It is the willingness and ability to do what is right—not what you or others think is right—and there is often a difference. Most people who have been brought up in the right surroundings know what is right, yet they hope they can get away with something—anything—and that their words and actions will remain forever locked in their own minds.

The question we must ask ourselves when we consider doing what is wrong versus what is right is: can I handle getting caught? Is the price worth it? How will I react to getting caught? Wouldn't it just be easier to deal in truth? All the time?

The answer is yes. So why do people misrepresent, lie, or tell little "innocent" fibs? I don't know. We are all guilty—at least one time in our lives and most of us several times—of shading the truth for what we feel is a justifiable cause. Is this wrong? I am not a moralist. But I do believe that character and integrity are related.

Here are a few simple questions to ask the next time you are considering being anything less than truthful:

1. What will I lose and gain by dealing in untruth?
2. Who will this lack of truth impact other than me?
3. Is it easy for me to shade the truth, and do I do it often? Why?
4. If I deal only in the truth—all the time—what will that do for me?

Turn It Around

Always deal in the truth, no matter what.

MISTAKE #15: *Getting Discouraged*

Have you ever wanted to quit anything? What was the cause of your discouragement? Was it a sense of loss? Feeling out of control? Loss of faith in yourself or the future? Was it feeling that your present circumstances would never end?

Whatever the cause, I can only tell you that this emotion, more than most other emotions, will drain your creativity, purpose, and resolve. Discouragement is a signal that something is wrong, something in your life needs to change. You can pay attention to its warning signs and find another way to approach whatever is causing your pain—or you can choose to whine, blame, or hide.

The one thing that has helped me more than any other is my faith in God and the knowledge that "this, too, shall pass." During difficult times, I have known deep in my soul and heart that what was happening was necessary for me in order to make a change in my life. It was life's way of guiding me to a better tomorrow. It was not meant to break me, but to show me a better path. For many years, I ignored this inner guidance, feeling that I could do everything on my own without help from anyone or anything. As I matured, however, I came to learn and accept that we all need help from someone sooner or later.

People will often let you down in your time of need. There is one guiding truth we all must learn if we are to overcome the feelings of loss of control: we are all on God's path to perfection, and we will all make mistakes traveling that path.

If you are discouraged today about anything, know that this discouragement is in your life for your higher good. I know that while you are in the depths of despair this is a difficult request, but it is one that I believe you must learn to accept with grace and gratitude.

Turn It Around
Remember that all things pass. Just relax.

MISTAKE #16: *Lacking Self-Discipline*

In life, we either pay the price of discipline or the price of regret. We pay these prices in all areas of our life: our careers, relationships, health, spiritual development, and financial affairs. It is unfortunate that many of us—yours truly included—fail to comprehend this simple law of life.

Let me explain. The laws that apply to all of life's issues—such as discipline, commitment, patience, integrity, practice, self-control, and focus—either help us live with freedom, peace, and harmony or heartache, failure, regrets, and misfortune as we move along the path of life. Much of the latter could be avoided (not all of it) if we would understand, accept, and integrate this simple truth into our lives.

The price of discipline is that daily dose of exercise, that moderation in our life affairs, our eating habits, our relationship strategies such as open and honest communication, and managing our resources wisely. The lack of these daily little disciplines accumulates day by day and year by year until each of us inherits the consequences of these misdeeds.

I have had many personal experiences where the daily lack of discipline came back to haunt me. I am discovering through these learning experiences that no one is immune to this truth. Arrogance, ignorance, or a combination of both is no excuse, and life really doesn't give a twit if you claim either. We pay one way or another. And discipline weighs ounces, while regret weighs tons.

The pain of discipline is nothing compared to the sting of regret.

Turn It Around

Remember, it is better to pay the price of discipline than regret.

MISTAKE #17: *Trying to Be Someone Else*

Being who you are is often a very difficult task. Managers, customers, spouses, friends, parents, and siblings often ask us directly or indirectly to behave in ways that are consistent with who they think we should be. For many years I have been accused of being a maverick. That word can mean many different things to each of us. I don't know whether I am one or not, but I do know that we can't be happy, successful, or at peace with ourselves or with the world as long as we are being anyone other than who we truly are. Yes, we are developing, growing, changing, and becoming, but all of this needs to be in accordance with our own inner drive.

When we allow others to determine who we should be, how we should behave, what we should believe, how we should feel—I know, I know, a lot of shoulds—but that is precisely the point. Who should determine who we are? This is not rocket science, my friends. It is really quite simple: as long as you let others determine your destiny, personality, behavior, feelings, etc., you will never be really happy or successful (no matter how you choose to define success), nor will you ever be at peace with yourself.

Who in your life is not happy with who you are or who you are becoming? How are they attempting to influence your evolution? Don't let them do it. I have caved in to other people many times in the past and have always regretted it.

I am not saying, don't change. I am only suggesting that when you do change, change when *you* are ready for a new you, for whatever reason. Being true to yourself—to your values, dreams, hopes, desires, needs, and so on—is one of the greatest gifts you can give to yourself and the rest of the world.

Turn It Around
Grow and change on your own terms, not those of others.

MISTAKE #18: *Lacking Honest Intent*

Intent is important, but your success comes from your actions—what you do. I believe it is important to have good intentions, but show me what a person does, and I will show you their real intent.

I know people who consistently say: "Some day I will..."

I have heard hundreds of times: "I would like to start my own business, but..."

I have observed thousands of people say they want to lose weight, but can't give up that last french fry or piece of carrot cake.

I have heard hundreds of commitments from people who said they would—call me back, meet me at noon for lunch, send me something, etc.—but never followed through.

I will bet you have had many of the same experiences. The real question is: are you guilty of any of them? I have been, many times. I said for years I wanted to lose weight and kept eating myself into oblivion.

I said I wanted to write a book for over five years before I wrote *Soft Sell* in 1981. (By the way, its sales are now over 500,000 copies worldwide and still going strong.)

A few questions for you:

1. Is your word your bond?
2. Do you make promises to pacify people?
3. Do you do what you say you will do?
4. Do you let little roadblocks keep you from taking positive action?
5. Do you vacillate on what you want to do and why?
6. Do you talk about doing things to see how other people will react?
7. Do you talk repeatedly about doing something in an attempt to convince yourself to actually do it?

Turn It Around
Do what you say you are going to do.

MISTAKE #19: *Letting Your Life Slip By*

There are a number of outstanding reasons to keep a journal. Let's name a few of them. They are easy to write in, don't take up lots of space, and are a great way to stimulate your thoughts and help you remember important experiences and events. A journal can also:

1. Help you avoid drastic errors in judgment
2. Increase your effectiveness
3. Improve your income
4. Help you learn from your failures
5. Improve your relationships
6. Help you achieve your goals
7. Keep you headed in the right direction
8. Improve your lifestyle
9. Help you learn from others
10. Help you find peace and happiness
11. Save you time
12. Help you have more fun
13. Capture valuable memories

If all that isn't enough to get you to consider starting and keeping a personal success journal, I don't know what will. I can only tell you from personal experience that keeping a record of my insights, thoughts, ideas, successes, mistakes, errors, achievements, and failures, and their causes has done more for my career than any other single activity.

What have you got to lose? It takes less than ten minutes a day to capture all of those important little day-by-day events, feelings, activities, and their consequences that, when revisited on a regular basis, can have a galvanizing impact on your career, relationships, and life.

Turn It Around
Start and keep a journal for your career success.

MISTAKE #20: *Being out of Balance*

One of the issues facing many people today is the ability to maintain a sense of balance in their lives. Unfortunately, it is impossible to have total balance in your life. There are too many demands, issues, problems, needs, goals, and people to deal with. It is possible, however, to have enough balance to reduce the stress in your life while enjoying many of the gifts life has to offer.

Several areas that we need to balance are family, work, finances, friends, social relationships, spirituality, self-development, physical well-being, personal interests, career interests, and fun. At any given time, you can be way out of balance: for example, when you start a new business or career, when you have your first child, or when you are in a new relationship. It is normal to devote more time and energy to these activities while ignoring some of the others. Problems arise when we stay out of balance in one area for a long period of time—say, working seven days a week for twenty-five years at the expense of your health, friends, and family.

What are some steps we can take if we are out of balance?

1. Spend time deciding what is really important in your life in the short and long term.
2. Share your goals, dreams, needs, and frustrations about being out of balance with the people who matter in your life.
3. Learn to set better priorities.
4. Say no more often.
5. Determine where you are out of balance and ask yourself why.
6. Spend time planning your days, weeks, months, and years.
7. Get up an hour earlier or go to bed an hour later.
8. Accept the fact that there are times in your life when you will be temporarily out of balance.
9. Simplify your life.

Turn It Around
Live the balanced life you want to live.

MISTAKE #21: *Lacking Patience*

Patience is a virtue. That's not so easy to see while you are waiting for a flight that is three hours late or a friend you are meeting for lunch who is thirty minutes late, or when life doesn't happen according to your personal schedule. One lesson life will teach you is the need for patience in all things, whether it's the behavior of your customers, or the frustrating traffic jam you encounter on the way to an appointment. Why not look at patience from a few different perspectives?

1. Patience tests your faith.
2. Patience tests your resolve.
3. Patience tests your level of trust.
4. Patience tests your level of understanding.
5. Patience tests your degree of acceptance.

Each of us is faced daily with people, circumstances, issues, and life that get in our face and ask, "What are you made of?" Each of us responds differently to these challenges when they appear. Some people cave in, while others strive on. Some get stronger, while others give up. Some people learn, while others point their finger elsewhere as the cause of their misfortune. Some people take responsibility for the quality of their life, while others see themselves as victims. Some people whine, while others get on with it.

Patience can be seen on the faces of people who do not let life's stressors make them go ballistic. These people flow with life: the good, the bad, and the ugly. They realize that life is a mix of all of this, and lacking patience is to expect life and everything in it to be perfect—all the time. Well, my friends, welcome to the real world—a world with imperfections, struggle, pain, success, failure, problems, achievements, old age, and anything else positive or negative you can name.

Turn It Around
Relax and enjoy the ride. Anything less could kill you.

MISTAKE #22: *Letting Sales Slumps Get You Down*

Every salesperson experiences a slump sometime in their career.

Let's first define what I call a sales slump. Perhaps you think that the only sign of a slump is a period of reduced sales success, regardless of its nature or length. It is not quite that simple. There are a number of ways a salesperson can be in a slump. Any salesperson, regardless of experience or length of service, can find himself having a difficult time with one or more of the sales process issues or elements addressed in this book. They are:

1. Controlling your attitudes
2. Effective prospecting
3. Tailored presentations
4. Asking for the business
5. After-sales service

Successful salespeople know that selling is a process and not an event. They have learned that their role is to create relationships that lead to sales. It is not just about moving products off the floor.

The key to long-term success for any salesperson is to manage all of the five elements in a consistent and positive way. What good is it in the long run to have great closing skills if you are never in the presence of good prospects? What good is it to have excellent products and services if you can't get appointments? What good is it to have a good prospect if you can't ask for the business? Notice, I didn't say ask for the order, but for the business.

You can experience a sales slump in any one of these areas. Regardless of the issue, the results will generally be the same. Low sales. Low margins. Lost customers. Vulnerability to competition. Cutting prices to get the business, and so on.

If you are experiencing a slump, you can't just look at the big picture. You must look carefully at your approach, strategies, strengths, and weaknesses in each of the five categories. You must learn to ask yourself the right questions if you hope to get accurate information that will help you out of this negative sales period. Knowing the characteristics and causes of the current situation will help you prevent future slumps.

Turn It Around

Recognize that there will always be ups and downs in your career.

MISTAKE #23: *Lacking Clear Goals*

There is one major reason for setting goals: goals give your life direction. Daily direction, weekly direction, and yearly direction.

Don't be attached to the outcomes—only the process. One example: diets. The key to achieving and maintaining your ideal weight is to not take in more than you can burn off. That's it, folks. Eating carrot cake every night and not exercising is moving in the wrong direction. You can't reach your ideal destination (your goal weight) if you travel in the wrong direction.

What direction are you moving in as you travel down the highways of your life? We are all on seven highways: financial, familial, spiritual, mental, professional, social, and physical. One of the biggest mistakes most people make as they travel into their future via each of these highways is to sacrifice one for another. Another common mistake is not understanding that avoiding one of the areas will cause an interruption in all of the other areas at some point in the future.

There are seminars, books, tapes, videos, and courses on how, why, and when to set goals. Some say write them down, some say commit them to memory. I am not going to take issue with any of these authors or speakers. I only ask you to consider one simple concept: are you moving daily in the direction that will land you where you want to be if life gives you enough time? If you are not, change course. *Now*. Our lives are nothing more than the accumulation of moments, days, weeks, and years. Destiny is the result of all of this daily stuff, so pay attention to it.

Turn It Around
Spend routine time in goal-setting activities.

MISTAKE #24: *Letting Your Ego Get in the Way*

The ego wants to make you look good, keep you in control, and manipulate people, events, and life. It needs for you to be right. If you want to be happy and successful, you need to control your ego, not the other way around.

People whose lives are ruled by their egos tend to be filled with conflict, anxiety, stress, frustration, disappointment, and emotional game-playing.

Blame, resentment, anger, fear, and guilt are just a few of the emotional tools these people use. They are rarely ever truly happy. They might have fame, power, wealth, good looks, and lots of toys, but most of them secretly know they are not really happy. Now, there are many people who have these achievements and do enjoy a happy existence, but it's not because of those things. They would be just as happy if they lost any or all of them.

Your soul wants what is your ultimate highest good. Your ego wants to look good, be in control, and protect itself. The ego tends not to like vulnerability and reality. This sets you up for hurt, pain, and rejection.

One way to see if your ego is out of control is to look at how much conflict, disappointment, and stress you have in your life. These are often good indicators of who is in charge—your ego or your heart. Your heart wants only to be happy, your ego wants you to be right.

One of the biggest problems for many people is making the eighteen-inch journey from living their life from their mind to living their life from their heart. How are you doing?

Turn It Around
Keep your ego out of the sales process.

MISTAKE #25: *Not Managing Your Stress*

Stress in life is normal. Everything causes stress. There are positive things like getting promoted, getting married, relocating, starting a business, winning the lottery, retiring, having a baby, and any number of such things that cause stress. There are also negative things such as failing, getting fired, getting a divorce, missing a deadline, having a baby, getting promoted, starting a business, winning the lottery, death of a loved one, and relocating. Did you notice that I repeated some of the items in each list? Not a mistake, folks. Stress is not about what is happening, but how you respond to those things.

Stressors are not positive or negative. A relocation can be positive for one person and negative for another, as can a promotion and all of the other things I mentioned, as well as other situations. How can the death of a loved one be interpreted as a positive stressor? Personally, I don't know of anyone who wishes for the death of a loved one. But I am confident that somewhere out there in this world there is someone who will be relieved when a sick relative finally passes away and their loved one no longer has to deal with the pain and humiliation that disease can sometimes bring.

Stress is not caused by events. If it were, everyone would have the same reaction or response to similar events, and we know that this isn't the case. Stress can kill you or keep you alive. Stress can and will destroy your happiness if you do not learn to accept the reality of life and all of its issues, problems, and challenges. The key to successfully managing the stressors in your life is to develop some practical routines that help reduce the impact of these on your emotional and physical well-being. Exercise, prayer, meditation, laughter, fun, and new routines are just a few of the things that can help us manage stress.

Turn It Around

Recognize that your reaction to stress is entirely up to you.

MISTAKE #26: *Lacking Confidence in Yourself*

If there is one character trait that stands above all the rest when it comes to increased success, it would be self-confidence. Granted, when we begin to list all of the traits necessary for success, we could fill a book. From Attitude to Zeal and everything in between. Some qualities are more important than others. Integrity certainly must be included, along with persistence, belief, resilience, and resolve.

Here, I would like to focus on self-confidence. Self-confidence gives you the ability to:

- Overcome obstacles
- Deal with rejection
- Overcome failure
- Deal with adversity
- Take risks

People who have a high degree of self-confidence can often be perceived as being arrogant, cocky, aloof, insensitive, and conceited—but these traits do not have to accompany self-confidence. People with some of these negative traits don't necessarily possess self-confidence. If you are already self-confident, be careful that it does not lead you into the trap of developing the negative traits mentioned above. If you lack self-confidence, what can you do?

1. Determine in what circumstances you lack confidence.
2. Find areas where you can act confidently and build on those.
3. Ask a simple question: when I lack confidence, what is it that I am afraid of?
4. Take small steps in the beginning of a new activity or project. You don't have to tackle the world in one bite.

Turn It Around
Improve yourself every day.

MISTAKE #27: *Living Outside-In*

Living inside-out means taking responsibility for your quality of life, successes, failures, achievements, outcomes, risks, happiness, financial position, lifestyle, relationships, etc. People who live outside-in turn the responsibility for their happiness, success, and failures over to someone or something outside of themselves. They blame the weather, government, their spouse, the economy, their company or organization, where they live, their parents—the list goes on and on.

We are in a crisis of responsibility in many parts of the world today. No one wants to take the responsibility for burning themselves with hot coffee, getting fired, going broke, experiencing a divorce. Everyone seems to want to point the finger elsewhere.

One of the discoveries I have made during the past forty years is that people who live inside-out have more, do more, and are happier, more productive, more successful, and more balanced than people who live outside-in. This doesn't mean that inside-out people live carefree lives without adversity, problems, risks, failures, and a variety of negative issues. What they do differently is understand their own role in the outcomes of their lives.

How are you doing today? Are you living from the inside-out or the outside-in? If you don't know, all you have to do to find out is pay attention to how you react to the bumps, curves, disappointments, and negative stuff. Inside-out people get just as many flat tires as outside-in people do, but watch the reaction and you can quickly tell who is who, even if it is you.

Turn It Around
Live inside-out.

MISTAKE #28: *Not Managing Expectations*

One of life's biggest frustrations is the unrealized expectations of other people's behavior. Why won't the people in my life act the way I think they should? They never will, so relax and let it go. You can never be happy if you are attached to the expectations or outcomes you have for other people, no matter who they are.

The execution of all behavior by others is in their hands, not yours. I am not implying here that you should never have expectations, just that if you want to spend a lot of time and energy being disappointed, expect others to do whatever you believe, feel, or think they should—according to your standards. Sooner or later everyone—yes, everyone—will let you down. I'm not being negative, just realistic.

Managing your expectations means understanding that everyone is doing the best they can with what they have learned thus far in life. We are all learning every day, either by accident, design, or on purpose. We are learning what life wants us to learn about life, relationships, people, business, and so on—now. Please keep in mind that most of the time people are not setting out deliberately to disappoint you, upset you, make you miserable, angry, fearful, or whatever; they are just being themselves. You have no right to expect another person to live their life according to how you believe they should. Yes, you can hope, ask, beg, and rant and rave until you are blue in the face, but in the end, people are who they are, believe what they believe, feel what they feel, and act consistently with all of these.

Managing expectations also requires that we learn to love others as they grow through the individual lessons that life throws in their path, in spite of our attitudes, feelings, or beliefs. They may not always act as we would, or as we think they should, but guess what? That's okay. Do you want to live your life according to others' expectations? I didn't think so!

Turn It Around
Let go of illusions.

MISTAKE #29: *Repeating the Same Mistakes*

One of my heroes, Ben Franklin, had a simple program for success, wealth, and happiness. As one of the people who shaped the United States in the 1700s, he put forward the following approach to achieving success in any area of your life. I felt so strongly about these virtues that I put them in chapter one of my bestseller *Soft Sell* over twenty years ago. I have not changed my mind. You might feel that one or more no longer apply in today's world; however, if that is your feeling, I would ask that you not disregard his message too quickly, but look just a little deeper into your belief system for your reasons.

What Franklin proposed was to take a total of thirteen virtues and live with each one for one week at a time, integrating it, applying it, thinking about it, and making it a part of your consciousness. At the beginning of the second week, move on to the next one and repeat the process. When you complete the thirteenth virtue, go back and begin the process again. During the course of a year, you will spend four weeks living and breathing each of the thirteen virtues. At the beginning of the next year, repeat the process again. You can't imagine the power of repetition and what it can do for your attitudes, behavior, and overall well-being. Here are his thirteen virtues:

1. Temperance—Eat not to dullness, drink not to elevation.
2. Silence—Speak not but what may benefit others or yourself.
3. Order—Let all your things have their places. Let each part of your business have its time.
4. Resolution—Resolve to perform what you ought. Perform without fail what you resolve.
5. Frugality—Make not expense but to do good to others or yourself; waste nothing.
6. Industry—Lose no time. Be always employed in something useful.
7. Sincerity—Use no hurtful deceit. Think innocently and justly.
8. Justice—Wrong none by doing injuries or omitting the benefits that are your duty.
9. Moderation—Avoid extremes.
10. Cleanliness—Tolerate no uncleanliness in body,

clothes, or habitation.

11. Tranquility—Be not disturbed by trifles or at accidents common or unavoidable.

12. Chastity—Rarely use venery [sex] but for health or offspring—never to dullness, weakness, or the injury of your own or another's peace or reputation.

13. Humility—Imitate Jesus and Socrates.

Another way to use this approach is to develop your own list. One of the ways I use this concept is in running my business. Each week I pull, at random, out of a jar labeled "This Week's Focus," one of thirteen activities written on a small piece of paper—such as Sell, Promote, Prospect, Write, etc. Why not create your own list of attitudes or behaviors that you want to become a routine part of your life? It works.

Turn It Around
Learn from your mistakes.

MISTAKE #30: *Seeing Problems as Negative*

One of my heroes, the late Norman Vincent Peale, once said, "There is only one group of people that doesn't have problems and they are all dead. Problems are a sign of life. So, the more problems you have, the more alive you are." I would add, "If you don't have any problems, maybe you are on the way out of here and you don't know it yet."

This can be perceived as just a tongue-in-cheek philosophy of life; however, it is closer to the truth than you might think. One thing you and I have both learned is that everyone has problems. Some people have relationship problems, others have financial ones; some face career challenges, others struggle with health problems; some have social troubles, while others face difficult business challenges. No one is immune to adversity in life.

The key to success, happiness, peace, and life balance is to accept problems as a part of the life process of becoming, learning, and growing. Failures, whiners, or victims see problems as life picking on them. Winners in life—regardless of their position, status, age, or circumstances—see problems and adversity as a catalyst to becoming better, stronger, wiser, and more aware of the reality of their lives.

Problems are not positive or negative; they are neutral. They are events. It isn't what is happening in your life that matters; it is how you choose to see it and what you do with it. Whether you perceive it as negative or positive is entirely up to you and your life outlook.

Learn to see the negatives as loving teachers in your life, bringing you the opportunity to get a clearer vision of where you may need attitude adjustments, improved thinking, or better skills.

Turn It Around
Learn from adversity.

MISTAKE #31: *Living in the Past or Future*

Life is lived in the present, one moment at a time, not in the past or future. Our futures and memories are created in all of our *now* moments. Living in the present means staying focused on what is happening now, not what happened yesterday or what may happen tomorrow.

People who focus on past mistakes, errors in judgment, words that were said with innocence, omission, and disappointment tend to bring a great deal of negative energy into the present.

People who focus on future expectations, desires, hopes, and "someday" dreams tend to miss the value, joy, and wonder of their present moments.

Everyone has "stuff." Neither you nor anyone else will ever be rid of it all. The key is to understand that you can't fix what happened yesterday, and you can't fix anything tomorrow. You fix everything *now*.

Learn to stay focused in the now. What you can do now. What you can say now. How you are feeling now. What you believe now. What you want to happen now.

Turn It Around

Stay focused in the present.

CHAPTER 2

PROSPECTING MISTAKES

Selling is a process.

One of the biggest problems for many salespeople is not understanding that selling is a process, not an event. Effective selling is not just closing the sale, better prospecting, or more effective sales presentations.

Although all of these are important in their own way, effective selling today means blending each of these together in such a way that the prospect trusts, believes, and respects you and your organization, and wants or needs your product or service to help them improve the quality of their life or business enterprise.

For many years traditional sales training focused on the "close of the sale" as the most important element. Then the '70s and '80s rolled around, and the hot topics were prospecting, qualifying, and getting to the key decision makers. In the '90s, the focus shifted to consultative selling. What will the next decade bring? Who knows for sure? What we do know now is that to sell successfully is only half of the task. The balance is keeping the business. Organizations spend millions of dollars annually to attract and sell new business. Then they lose it for any number of reasons and have to replace it. So the saga continues.

Selling is about finding good potential prospects who can benefit from your products or services, persuading them to buy from you, and then maintaining positive relationships with them that ensure repeat and referral business as well as positive references. Are you focusing on only one particular aspect of the sales process as you sell? Are you weak in any particular part?

Each element of the process is intricately related to all the others. For example, let's take prospecting. If you have a poor prospect, it will be difficult to give them a solid sales presentation. It will be impossible to overcome their sales objections, and as for closing the sale—forget it.

How about the attitude issues in the sales process? Let's say you lack confidence in the quality of your products. That will affect your willingness to find new prospects. If you do find some, it will impact your ability to give a confident sales presentation. And so on.

How about one more? Let's say you have a fear of rejection. That will impact your willingness to ask questions, qualify your prospects, and discuss sales presentation issues that may be perceived as less than ideal. And asking for the order? Not in this lifetime.

I am sure you see my point. If you are going to sell successfully, you can't improve just one aspect of the sales process. You can't make up for poor prospecting with tricky closes. You can't make up for poor product knowledge with fancy footwork.

Since the skill of prospecting is the skill that ultimately contributes to success or failure, it's the best place to begin taking a look at the mistakes salespeople make in this area.

Remember, you will never turn a poor prospect into a customer with a great product or service, good presentation, or tricky close. However, a well-qualified prospect will help you sell them. One of the weakest areas of poor salespeople is the skill of prospecting. Master this, and the rest of the sales process will take care of itself.

"Face adversity promptly and without flinching, and you will reduce its impact."

—Winston Churchill

MISTAKE #32: *Selling Only by the Numbers*

For years, sales managers and sales trainers have been saying that sales is a "numbers" game. I can recall my first sales manager telling me over thirty-five years ago, "If you see enough people, you will make enough sales." First of all, what's enough sales? Second of all, how many is enough people? Thirdly, is this the best approach to take when prospecting for new business?

If you see enough qualified people, you will make enough sales. It isn't just the number, folks; it is focusing on prospects who qualify for your product or service. Now this doesn't mean that you should see fewer prospects. I am only suggesting that focusing on the numbers alone will guarantee failure sooner or later. Why? The more people you see, the more you will tend to see poor prospects; thus, more rejection. The average salesperson can't handle the amount of rejection that comes with this philosophy. This is why so many people become discouraged and fail or quit.

Think about it for just a minute. You see or call twenty-five prospects a week. You close one out of every five. That means you wasted time on twenty poor prospects.

But how do you know if they are poor prospects until you see or spend time with them? What if you took the time you spent with the twenty poor prospects and spent it with more good prospects—or even cultivating the five sales you made for repeat or referral business? Maybe your closing ratio could be one-third or even one-half.

Here is a real winner for success. Do both. See and call more prospects but—here's the difference—make sure they are qualified before you give them too much of your time and energy.

Turn It Around
Prospecting is not about how many people you see, but about the quality of the prospect.

MISTAKE #33: *Selling at the Wrong Level*

A common mistake salespeople make is failing to recognize the level at which they should be selling. There are five possible levels where you can direct your energy and time in the sales process:

1. *The product or service level.* This is where the salesperson focuses primarily on the price or features of the product or service and defines the product as a commodity. The salesperson's typical approach in this phase is to lower the price due to a prospect's price resistance or competitive pressure.

2. *The transaction level.* This is where the salesperson sees the sales process in traditional terms: prospecting, presentation, overcoming objections, and closing the sale. In most cases, this approach still tends to focus on the process rather than the customer.

3. *The solution level.* This is where the salesperson brings a solution to the prospect or customer for their specific problem or need. Although this is better than selling at the transaction level, it still

focuses on the relationship between the customer's needs and the features and benefits of the product or service.

4. *The relationship level.* Now we are getting more long-term-customer focused. Selling at this level requires patience, research, knowledge of the customer's short- and long-term agendas, time, effort, and a willingness to walk away from those sales where there is not a clear win-win outcome.

5. *The stakeholder or shared fate level.* Very few salespeople sell at this level. This is where, if your customer loses in any way, either directly or indirectly related to your product or service, you also lose.

Turn It Around
See effective selling not as a transaction, but as a process of building relationships.

MISTAKE #34: *Being a Victim of Sales Cycles*

Many products and services have different sales cycles, from the first prospect meeting to the close of the sale. Some cycles can be several months to a few years. Some can be just a few days or a few hours.

Many salespeople believe that they are not in control of the sales cycle. They put the buying control into the hands of the prospect. Keep in mind that people buy when they are ready to buy, not when you need to sell.

First of all, remember that you do not change the prospect's buying needs, timetable, readiness, or urgency. You discover them. If your prospect has just signed a three-year contract with a competitor, guess what? This is not a prospect for you until he begins to consider renewing or changing suppliers.

Most sales cycles are not etched in stone. They are a function of your ability to get to the real issues, needs, pain, and problems of your prospect. If you fail to identify these accurately, you will most likely never create the sense of urgency necessary to close sales sooner rather than later.

Don't get yourself into a mental rut that insists your sales cycle always has to be eight weeks, or six months, or seven days, or whatever. I'll bet those of you who believe that your normal buying cycle is, let's say, six months have closed sales in less time than that as well as more. The point is that the cycle is not a predetermined period of time. It is a function of your ability to identify critical prospect issues and then show the prospect how you can satisfy in a way that is acceptable.

Turn It Around

Create a sense of buying urgency to control sales cycles.

MISTAKE #35: *Thinking People Buy from People They Like*

Has selling really changed all that much in the past fifty years? Those of you who have been selling for less than five years most likely will answer that question with a *no*. Those of you with battle scars going back into the '60s, '70s, and even the '80s may answer with a resounding *yes*. Others of you just are not sure how much things have changed at all or can't articulate it.

Some things have changed. Some have not. What has changed from my perspective of over forty-five years of selling and teaching sales? Here are a few:

1. People have better, quicker, and easier access to information about your products or services and those of your competitors.
2. People want you to help them make better-informed decisions.
3. There are now three major segments of prospects: millions of Baby Boomers, millions of retired folks, and millions of people under the age of thirty-five who have lots and lots of money.

4. There are fewer layers of management to go through to get to your decision-maker.
5. Technology is changing buying patterns and attitudes.
6. People will not tolerate poor quality or poor service. They will do business with your competitor.
7. Your prospects have an increasing number of options, choices, and vendors from whom to purchase.

How about what hasn't changed?

People buy from people they trust.

Stop trying to get people to like you. Get them to trust you.

Turn It Around
Focus on establishing and building trust, not on being liked.

MISTAKE #36: *Ignoring Past Clients*

Lost business is not necessarily lost forever. Many salespeople neglect this lucrative source of new business. I say new because if you treat these past customers as new prospects, you may just regain their business. There are a number of reasons why customers leave you. Some of them are:

1. They were wooed away by a competitor promising better prices, better service, or some other benefit.
2. Their organization has changed, and new management is not aware of the strengths of your services or products because this information was not passed on to them by their predecessors.
3. You or your organization failed to deliver as promised.
4. You or your organization let trust and/or respect erode in the relationship.
5. There is some hidden reason, such as they have a relative in the business that they deal with now, have lost buying authority, or are leaving their organization for another position.

There are others, but these are some of the ones you can control.

What can you do to regain this business?

1. First, you must learn the *real* reason why the customer left.
2. You have to be willing to begin again.
3. You need to work as hard to keep the business as you did to get it.
4. You must reassess where you went wrong. Was it an issue of price, service, quality, distribution, arrogance, ignorance, or interest in keeping the business, or was it some other major or minor mistake?
5. You must keep in touch with previous customers.

Turn It Around

Stay in touch with previous customers.

MISTAKE #37: *Staying in Your Comfort Zone*

Over time, it can become easy to get stuck in one of a number of comfort zones when it comes to behavior, performance, techniques, or attitudes. Let's look at a few of the common ones to which many salespeople fall prey.

1. Calling only on clients or customers that you like or that like you
2. Selling only the products or services you make the most money on, know the most about, or are easiest to sell
3. Slowing down your sales activities at certain times of the month or year
4. Adjusting your performance once you have exceeded your quota or your manager's expectations
5. Avoiding new applications of your products or services
6. Spending too much time with customers with whom you have a lot in common despite their limited purchasing potential

7. Having nonproductive routines that keep you away from the real role of selling
8. Spending too much time in after-sales service issues that keep you from selling more to new prospects

List some of the areas in which you feel you are being locked in a comfort zone. After you have completed your personal list, answer the following:

1. How long have you had this behavior or attitude?
2. How is it sabotaging your sales success?
3. If continued, how will it impact your career (in the short and the long term)?
4. What can you do to change it?

Turn It Around
Be willing to try new and creative approaches to prospecting.

MISTAKE #38: *Letting Lost Business Go without a Fight*

We all lose business. Some salespeople who lose a sale or a customer go into various irrational emotional reactions: they blame someone or everyone, make excuses, sulk, get angry, or run and hide. Successful salespeople understand the ebb and flow of business and relationships. If you have good sales skills, a good product or service, a positive attitude, and a good prospect—sooner or later you will sell them.

Here are a few suggestions to use when you do lose a sale:

1. Follow up with a thank-you note or letter.
2. Follow up with an after-sales critique or evaluation.
3. Follow up with additional sources or proof—testimonials, articles, etc.
4. Find out what your competitor did better than you to get the business.
5. Don't assume it was price, even if that is what they tell you.
6. Don't let it negatively affect your attitude. Keep at it.

This week's lost business can be next month's sale. This month's lost customer can become next year's home run. You will win some and you will lose some. You won't win them all, and you won't lose them all. Just remember: staying power over the long haul is much more beneficial than quick short-term success.

Turn It Around

Have a specific strategy for dealing with lost business.

MISTAKE #39: *Not Routinely Networking*

There is a cliché that says, "It isn't what you know, but who you know that counts in the development of your career or business." I would like to change it to: "It isn't who you know, but who knows about you or your organization."

You can know a lot of people, but if they don't know a great deal about you, the value of these contacts is limited. One of the keys to effective networking is the ability to both accumulate a variety of contacts in your database and make these people aware of your skills, abilities, interests, and needs.

I have met tens of thousands of people in my forty-five-year career, but I would guess that fewer than five hundred can contribute to my success in some way by being able to introduce me to others they know who might be potential clients for me.

Networking is finding people who may be a center of influence for you, then taking the opportunity to get to know them, and giving them the opportunity to get to know you. Most salespeople are really poor net-workers. They fail to join organizations where the people who could benefit them congregate, or if they do belong, they fail to get involved or even participate in various meetings and networking opportunities.

How are you as a networker? Do you promote yourself with regularity in areas where influential people mingle? Do you belong to industry associations and attend some of their meetings? Do you keep a database of contacts—where you met them and how they might be of value to you? Do you have some method to keep in touch with them (like a newsletter, periodic notes, telephone calls, or emails)?

Turn It Around
Develop a regular routine for finding and meeting new people who can help you.

MISTAKE #40: *Asking, "Did You Get the Information I Sent?"*

Customers and prospects have a great deal on their plates today. They have the demands of customers, bosses, fellow staff members, suppliers, and a variety of organizational, departmental, and industrial issues that take a great deal of time and energy. When salespeople call on these busy prospects or clients, they must realize that what they are selling is not the most important thing in that prospect's life. Although the product or service might be of interest and value to the clients, salespeople must also do their essential follow-up. Why don't salespeople follow up? Or when they do follow up, why do they say dumb things like, "Did you get the literature I sent?" Here's why:

1. They fear a "no" or a rejection.
2. They know the prospect is not going to buy.
3. They believe the prospect is too busy to talk with or see them.
4. They believe their competitors are going to get the business anyway.
5. They don't have an effective follow-up strategy.
6. They have nothing else to say.

7. They knew they had a poor prospect anyway, so they figure, "Why bother?"

Are you guilty of any of these? It is easy to fall into the no-follow-up trap. Here are a few ideas to consider when you next follow up a sales call:

1. Don't begin with a closed-ended question like, "Have you made a decision yet?" Instead ask, "Where are you in the decision process?"
2. Don't ask, "Did you get the information that I sent?" Instead ask, "What is your impression of the information that I sent?"
3. Don't ask, "When can we get together to discuss our next step?" Instead say, "Let's get together next Monday to..."
4. Don't ask, "Do you have any question about the proposal?" Instead ask, "Is there anything in the proposal that would prevent us from getting this order started?"

Turn It Around
Develop an effective follow-up strategy and use it.

MISTAKE #41: *Being Afraid of Rejection*

What is the number one cause of failure in sales? The inability to overcome the fear of rejection. Why do people let this fear negatively influence their behavior? Here are a few thoughts to consider:

1. Not everyone you try to sell to will want to buy from you.
2. Expecting everyone you meet to like or accept you is to live in fantasyland.
3. If you don't ask for something—anything—it is unlikely you will ever get it.
4. Does fear of rejection prevent you from asking probing questions, asking for an appointment, or asking for the order?
5. The fear of rejection is an attitude issue and can be overcome only by strengthening other attitudes—such as confidence, self-belief, patience, trust, and self-image.
6. The fear of rejection is symptomatic of a need for acceptance.

Does the fear of rejection ever prevent you from:

1. Picking up the phone and making that next call?
2. Asking for the business?
3. Asking difficult probing questions?
4. Asking for referrals?
5. Asking for a bigger order?
6. Asking for a letter of testimony?
7. Asking for more responsibility in your position or for a raise?
8. Following up on a customer who has had a problem?
9. Asking for an appointment with an important person?
10. Asking for a deposit?
11. Asking for a long-term contract?

Turn It Around
Ask. If you don't, you may never receive.

MISTAKE #42: *Not Practicing on Good Prospects*

How much time do you spend practicing and developing your skills? Do you practice a new technique on a prospect or do you try it out on a fellow salesperson or your supervisor first? Do you not practice at all and just show up? Show me any athlete in any sport who achieves success, fame, or even makes a decent living, and I will show you someone who spends more time practicing than performing. Here are a few examples.

Olympic athletes spend in excess of three thousand hours preparing for a two-, three-, or ten-minute race. Most professional golfers hit hundreds of golf balls every day to refine their swing, balance, and performance. Baseball, basketball, or football teams practice for several hours three to five days a week, every week, for one two- or three-hour game. Are other careers different? No. Doctors, contractors, teachers, and counselors spend time in research, discovery, and experimentation. They don't wait until they get into the operating room or in front of the classroom. I spend a minimum of two to three hours in preparation for every hour in front of an audience.

Show me someone in any discipline who just shows up, and I will show you someone who is average at best, never makes a difference, and seldom achieves greatness. How about salespeople? What can they practice before a sales call? A telephone call? Much more:

1. New questions to ask prospects
2. New ways to ask those questions
3. How to cover the benefits of a product or service feature
4. How to create a sense of urgency
5. How to professionally terminate a presentation on a poor prospect
6. How to increase a sale by "up-selling"
7. How to better answer a prospect's questions

Turn It Around
Practice new techniques on a fellow salesperson.

MISTAKE #43: *Talking Too Much*

One of the biggest mistakes poor salespeople make is talking too much. Another is giving information before they get it. When you make these mistakes, you will tend to turn off most potential customers or clients.

A product- or organization-driven sales approach puts your focus on giving information rather than getting it. A customer-driven presentation is one in which you get more information than you give, and the information you give is what the prospect needs or wants to hear, not what you want to tell them.

The key to your success is not in the delivery of a preplanned message that covers all the features that some genius in your organization has decided are important. The key to your success is to discover your prospect's needs, issues, concerns, problems, wants, desires, and attitudes. Then deliver only the information that they need in order to make an intelligent buying decision now. Give them the rest of the stuff later—if they want it.

When you talk too much, you will give unnecessary or wrong information. Learn to let the prospect drive the process—not the control of it, but the information portion.

There is an outdated sales axiom which states, "Plan your sales calls."

If you have been selling your product or service for a year or more, you shouldn't need to plan the information you are going to give. Instead, plan the information you need to get and the questions you are going to ask.

Turn It Around

The prospect should be talking at least twice as much as you are.

MISTAKE #44: *Losing Control of the Sales Process*

There are many ways salespeople lose control of the sales process. Here are a few:

1. They quote price—usually because the prospect has asked—before they have had a chance to build value.
2. They don't ask enough questions early in the sales process. They just ramble on.
3. They send out literature when asked without first qualifying the prospect.
4. They don't get deposits and hope the prospect will pay someday.
5. They leave "will calls" (call-me-back voice mails) when telephoning a prospect.

Control is one of the key elements for success in sales. Successful salespeople understand that control is not manipulation but is in the ultimate best interests of the prospect or client. I'll bet you have a prospect right now, as you are reading this, with whom you have lost control. You are waiting for this prospect to respond to your offer or appeal. How do you get and keep control? The best time to get control of the sales process with a new prospect is in the early stages of the relationship. It is very difficult to get it back later. One of the best strategies is to resist the tendency to jump from information-getting to information-giving in the presentation.

Successful salespeople determine not only the buying habits and payment philosophy of the prospects and clients they have, but also the respect they receive and the manner in which they are treated by these prospects and clients. Some of you probably have some clients you wish you didn't have, right? Pay attention to early signals and remember that you and I have what our prospects want and need: solutions to their needs and problems. So keep control of the buying process.

Turn It Around
Keep control with a planned approach.

MISTAKE #45: *Acting like You Need the Business*

Sounding pathetic is one of the surest ways to ensure that your customer will lack confidence and respect for both you and your organization. People buy when they are ready to buy, not when you need to sell. It is essential that in every sales situation that you always put the prospect or customer ahead of your needs.

Begging is not attractive.

You beg when you say things like:

- "What time is convenient for you?" Instead try, "Let's see if we can arrange a mutually beneficial time."
- "We're the best in the business." Instead say, "Let's see how our product or service will solve your problem."
- "When can you let me know your decision?" Instead say, "Let's set a time to discuss your decision."
- "Can I call you in a few weeks to follow up?" Instead promise, "I'll call you in a few weeks to discuss your questions and further interest."

- "We can't do that. It's against company policy." Instead say, "Let's see how we can accomplish this."

There are thousands of ways to sound insecure and unprofessional. All of them send the message that you lack confidence in your credibility and your ability to perform.

Turn It Around
Keep the focus on how the customer benefits.

MISTAKE #46: *Not Building Trust Early*

I asked earlier, "Has selling really changed all that much in the past fifty years?"

Well, some things have changed, and others have not. My forty-five–plus years of experience in selling and teaching sales has given me great perspective on this. Here are a few things that have changed:

1. People have better, quicker, and easier access to information about your products and services, and those of your competitors.
2. People want you to help them make better-informed decisions.
3. More women are in positions of influence.
4. There are increased opportunities to sell to people from different cultures.
5. There are fewer layers of management to go through to get to your decision maker.
6. Technology is changing customer buying patterns and attitudes.
7. Your prospects have an increasing number of options, choices, and vendors from whom to purchase.

How about what hasn't changed?

1. People still buy what they want and desire.
2. People still want a fair value.
3. People do not want to be lied to or misled.
4. People do not want to pay too much to solve their problem or satisfy their wants and needs.
5. People buy from people they trust.

Turn It Around

Establish the prospect's trust before you begin to sell.

MISTAKE #47: *Not Asking Elevator Questions*

What are elevator questions? Let me answer by asking you a question: if you were told by a prospect that you had sixty seconds to sell them, what would you do? Would you condense your sales message into a one-minute presentation, or talk about your organization and its strengths and history? Would you ask a few thought-provoking questions, or stand there dumbfounded, wondering what to do or what to say next?

I recently met a prospect on an elevator in a Las Vegas hotel at a speaking engagement. He looked like he was a business-type person so I asked him, "What do you do for a living?" He responded, "I am in the insurance industry." My follow-up question was, "What do you do in the insurance business?" He said he was the president. (Keep in mind, I didn't have a lot of time since we were on an elevator.)

Then came my Elevator Question: "Do you know what your lost sales are costing you every year?"

He paused, then answered, "I am not sure. What do you do for a living?"

I said, "I am in the business of helping organizations reduce their lost sales revenue." (Elevator Statement.)

An elevator question is any question that cuts to the heart of your prospect's challenges, concerns, or fears to make them think. It's a question that implies that you or your organization may have a possible solution for their problems. Remember that elevator questions are not used only on elevators. They can be used at social settings, while selling on the telephone, or anywhere in the sales process. All of the great salespeople I have ever met or had in my audiences were masters at elevator questions.

Turn It Around
Develop several urgency-building, probing elevator questions.

MISTAKE #48: *Not Getting to the Decision-Maker*

One of the biggest time-wasters in sales is when salespeople fail to get to the real decision-makers and present their products or services to people who cannot say yes or can only say no. Since many organizations are undergoing sweeping changes in management and in the way they purchase from vendors, it is increasingly difficult to identify who is really in charge. I am not suggesting that, at certain times in the sales process, it is inappropriate to give a presentation to someone who can only recommend your products. I do suggest you keep in mind that every time you present to a non-decision-maker, you lose an important ingredient in the sales process: control.

There are two prospecting strategies you can follow when dealing with decision-makers: bottom-up or top-down prospecting. In bottom-up, you start anywhere in the organization where someone will see you. In top-down, you begin with the senior person and work down. I have found that, once you have identified a prospect as qualified, the best approach is both top-down and bottom-up simultaneously. The bottom-up portion is the easier of the two. It is here that you gather additional knowledge about needs, wants, current suppliers, and other pertinent information. Top-down is where you sell the big picture.

When I call a new prospect, I ask the contact, "Who is the person in your organization making the buying decision about x?" My next question is, "Who is that person's supervisor?" The next step is easy. I say thank you and call back and ask for the supervisor. It could be the president, senior VP, or CEO; it doesn't matter. I am looking for the ultimate decision-maker at that location, branch, division, subsidiary—whatever. Without getting to the ultimate economic buyer, you are only logging sales calls that may never go anywhere.

Turn It Around
Give presentations only to those who make buying decisions.

MISTAKE #49: *Not Knowing Your Competitors*

Many salespeople tend to see their competition as only those businesses selling a similar product, service, or idea. In other words, salespeople selling computers tend to see their competitors as other computer stores, retailers, or manufacturers. In reality, people selling insurance, travel, furniture—you name it—need to know that their competition is not just their direct competitors, but anyone and everyone who is trying to get a piece of the corporate or consumer dollar.

I can recall years ago, when I was just beginning my career as a speaker and trainer, I lost my first big sales training contract to a salesperson selling computer hardware. In my sales approach, I strategically positioned my features and benefits so that any other speaker or trainer would have difficulty successfully competing with me. Problem was, though I was successful at keeping my fellow speakers and trainers at bay, I ultimately lost the sale to someone who was selling something totally unrelated to training. I asked myself, *Where did I go wrong?*

It was simple: I only saw people who sold what I was selling as my competitors. Wrong. My prospect, the company president, told me that the training program I was selling was important to him and that he would keep it on the back burner for the short-term. Upgrading all of their computer hardware was more important to him at that time.

So, what's the solution? If you are going to continue to succeed and prosper in sales, you have to be better, smarter, quicker, more flexible, and more resilient than every salesperson in your territory, no matter what they sell. Just being better than the people selling similar products is not enough.

Turn It Around
Learn everything about all of your competitors.

MISTAKE #50: *Failing to Build Psychological Debt*

One of my early lessons in sales happened over forty years ago. I was getting lots of feedback like, "Tim, you are really good at this." "You are going to be really successful in this business." "You really know your stuff." Kind words, yes. But sales? No. I went to a good friend who was making over a million dollars a year selling insurance and told him of my plight: lots of compliments, no orders. This is, as best as I can recall, his advice:

"Tim, when you give a sales presentation to a prospect, are you nice to them? Do you give them your time? Do you educate them? Do you give them the benefit of your experience?" My answers to all of his questions were yes.

He replied, "Here is what is happening. You are building a psychological debt. They owe you, and the way they pay off the debt is with a compliment. Once you accept the compliment, the debt is paid." Thus, no order.

Well, I couldn't feed my kids compliments, so I said, "Larry, what do I do?" His response: "Refuse their compliments. You see, when you do not accept the compliments, the debt still exists."

"How do I do that, Larry?"

"Say to your prospect something like, 'If I were that good, we would be doing business together." Or, "If I am going to be successful, I need to be better able to communicate the benefits of my proposal to you. I am sorry, but I don't deserve that compliment." He continued, "Now, when you get a compliment and an order, say 'Thank you very much.'" This one piece of advice helped more in my sales career than dozens of the books I read and seminars I attended. Don't let your prospect off the psychological hook that easily. What you want and need is business, not validation, approval, acceptance, or appreciation.

Turn It Around
Create psychological debt through service.

MISTAKE #51: *Lacking a Precise Call-Back Approach*

Earlier I introduced the subject of failing to do the essential follow-up (see Mistake #41). Over the years, when I have followed up with a prospect who has been considering my services, I have heard more often than I can state, "Thanks for getting back to me. I had every intention of calling you, but have just been too busy. Let's get this program rolling." Why don't salespeople follow up? And what are the benefits of an effective follow-up strategy? Taking the time to follow up and having an effective follow-up strategy are two critical issues that will determine the success of salespeople. What are some more reasons salespeople don't follow up?

1. They are too disorganized and are not even aware that they should follow up.
2. They lack confidence in themselves or their organization and its services or products.
3. They believe their competitors are going to get the business anyway.

If you are guilty of any of these, here are a few ideas to consider for your next follow-up sales call:

1. Don't open with a closed-ended question like, "Have you made a decision yet?" Instead ask, "Where are you in the decision process?"
2. Don't ask, "Did you get the information that I sent?" Instead try, "What is your impression of the information that I sent?"
3. Don't ask, "When can we get together to discuss our next step?" Instead suggest, "Let's get together next Monday to…"

What, then, are the benefits of an effective follow-up strategy?

1. You'll see increased sales.
2. You'll look more professional.
3. You'll beat the competition.

Turn It Around
Have an effective follow-up strategy.

MISTAKE #52: *Not Asking for Referrals*

It is easier, less stressful, less costly, and less time-consuming to sell to qualified referrals than to any other source of prospects. It is amazing how many salespeople fail to make asking for referrals a regular part of their selling behavior. Getting referrals is not rocket science. Although there are several methods to generate referral business, the best way I know of is to just ask.

I have surveyed my sales audiences for over twenty-five years by asking them, "How many would like to have more referrals?" I always get a unanimous show of hands. My next question is, "Why don't you have them?" and the answer is always, "I don't ask." Referrals can come from anywhere: customers, non-competing salespeople or suppliers, friends, relatives, your banker, or your neighbor.

There is no wrong time to ask for referrals. Many salespeople feel that to ask for referrals from customers, they must have first provided the service or product in a satisfactory way. Why wait to ask? Every minute you are not creating a referral-awareness in the minds of your customers or other sources is one more minute your competitors might be one step ahead of you.

Timing is important in selling. Every minute you lose discovering a new prospect that will benefit from your product or service brings you closer to missing out on additional business.

Don't wait. There are several ways to generate referrals. You can call, write, email, fax, or visit a customer for the sole purpose of asking for referrals. Set some specific goals to generate a certain number of referrals every week for the next several weeks until the habit is a permanent part of your regular selling routine.

Turn It Around
Ask every customer and prospect for referrals.

MISTAKE #53: *Not Using a Prospect Profile*

Prospecting has two basic elements: identification and qualification.

Identification is finding potential customers who have the need, desire, and ability to pay for your products or services, the willingness to see you, and who can either make the buying decision or contribute significantly toward it.

Qualification is: a) the strategies used to determine which of the prospects you have identified are the best prospects in whom to invest your time, energy, and resources, and b) discovering the information needed to develop a sales strategy and approach that will enable you to tailor your presentation to the needs, desires, problems, concerns, and buying style of your prospect.

If you sell a product or service to the general consumer, the identification process can be a time-consuming and difficult one. Of the thousands of people you could see, which ones—from a cursory first look—would make it past the qualification process?

If you sell to the business community, health care industry, government, or any other major business segment—whether regionally, nationally, or globally—the identification process is as easy as perusing a directory, custom database, or specific mailing list for those prospects that meet your general criteria.

A system I have used successfully for over forty-five years is to build an ideal prospect profile. This is developed by evaluating the characteristics of your best customers and then creating a profile or template that you work towards while both identifying and qualifying each potential prospect for as close a match to that profile as possible.

Turn It Around

Use a systematic method for qualifying prospects.

MISTAKE #54: *Not Becoming a Resource*

In a highly competitive international business climate, it is essential that salespeople become even more creative in finding ways to service their clients. One principle to keep in mind is that it is easier, less stressful, less time-consuming, and less expensive to do more business with a present client than it is to keep looking for new clients.

One of the best ways I have discovered to reduce client turnover and generate repeat business, referrals, and the opportunity to use the client as a reference is to be a better resource for your client. A newsletter is one example of a resource that clients might appreciate. Here's another: recently I have sent three articles to other authors on a variety of topics that I thought would interest them. My cost: around $1 per mailing. The return: additional business, referrals, and references. Find ways to be a better resource for your customers and watch your business grow. Here are some examples to get you started:

1. Send articles that you think will interest your client.

2. Send books and audio tapes that will contribute to their knowledge.
3. Conduct training seminars for their employees.
4. Keep them abreast of industry trends, forecasts, and competitive information.
5. Bring them business.
6. Give them a subscription to a publication in an area that interests them.
7. Provide your home and mobile telephone numbers.
8. Be willing to go the extra mile. Promise a lot and deliver more.
9. Send special greeting cards for birthdays, business anniversaries, or other notable days.
10. Share any information with your customers that will contribute to their success.

Turn It Around
Be a business resource for all of your customers.

CHAPTER 3

SALES PRESENTATION MISTAKES

I recall that in my first sales position, we were trained by a national organization, a leader in its industry, to "memorize" the sales presentation. We were then instructed to go out and tell the company story, giving the presentation we had learned. That industry at the time had a 95 percent turnover ratio of new salespeople in the first year.

I was one of those in the 95 percent who was let go. No wonder. Don't sell anything for six months and you might begin to think you should have taken up another career. Well, I went back into the same business and within one year was an industry leader. How?

Simple: I changed my focus from selling my company and its strengths and product features to determining my prospect's needs, wants, and desires.

But beware. Selling today has, in many cases, become like a giant shell game, or what I refer to as the Big Pow Wow. For those of you who haven't got a clue as to what I am talking about, let me explain. Years ago, when the white man invaded the Native Americans' homeland, they would often bring gifts. These gift exchanges were accomplished with various ritualistic behaviors on the part of both parties. When all was said and done, if the white man escaped with his head, it was a good day. Both parties were selling. The Native Americans were selling the right to trespass, hunt, or even live; and the white invaders, their goods and trinkets from the East.

Flash forward two hundred fifty years and what have we got? You and I are trading what we have (the product or service we provide, that our customer wants or needs) for their wampum (money).

Some Native Americans, without the benefit of attending the latest seminar on effective negotiation, were quite persuasive when it came to getting more of what they wanted. The white men often walked away, after giving a great deal, with the feeling that they had been taken to the cleaners. Today, many salespeople give away far too much—in the way of margins, discounts, and extra services—to satisfy the demands or expectations of the prospect. They treat the sales process like a big shell game or old-fashioned Pow Wow.

Customers today want value, not trinkets; service, not empty words; honest commitments, not temporary involvement; and fair treatment, not selfish demands.

In an age where competition abounds, choices are increasing, and quality, service, and timely communication are the hallmarks of positive relationships, salespeople can no longer afford to live with the illusions that they can get by with giving World Series tickets, dinners at expensive restaurants, or special gifts. People are as smart now as they were two hundred years ago, maybe even smarter.

Be careful not to fall into the trap of giving away more than is necessary. Most customers today would much rather have a fair price, good value, and professional treatment than all of this other "stuff."

If you want to ride off into the sunset with your head where it belongs—on top of your shoulders—become familiar with what your customers really want, not what you think they want, or what they may even tell you they want.

"The first ingredient in communication is truth, the second, good sense, the third, good humor, and the fourth, wit."

—Sir William Temple

MISTAKE #55: *Not Giving Tailored Presentations*

One of the biggest mistakes poor salespeople make is talking too much. They launch into a "feature dump" covering a litany of features, but a truly persuasive sales presentation is nothing more than a conversation with a specific agenda. It is a process of discovering what your prospects want, need, and are concerned about, and relating these to the particular aspects of your product or service.

If you have four sales appointments today, each presentation should be totally different. The structure might be similar, but the content should be specific to the customer. A good sales presentation:

1. Is brief and focused
2. Comes from the prospect's perspective—not yours or the organization's
3. Is an interactive, two-way conversation
4. Blends the right amount of emotional appeal (customer benefits) with logical reasons to buy (features and product benefits)

5. Involves the prospect, allowing them to develop some ownership of and comfort with the product or service

6. Ties the customer benefits back to their dominant emotional buying motive (see Mistake #65 for more on dominant emotional buying motives)

7. Tests the attitudes or acceptance of the prospect with assumptive phrases and trial closes

8. Approaches the prospect from their personality, style, and comfort level

9. Is tailored, tailored, tailored

An effective sales presentation is not an "unloading" of information on the prospect. Remember, if a prospect knows what you sell and will see you, he will buy. If he doesn't, it is because you missed something!

Turn It Around
Tailor each presentation to the client's specific desires.

MISTAKE #56: *Not Having a Concise Defining Statement*

A defining statement is a very specific and precise clarifying statement. It combines all of the necessary ingredients so that when a prospect walks away from an elevator conversation with you, he knows who you are, what you do, and how he will benefit by doing business with you.

A defining statement should include all of the following ingredients:

1. *It must use common words that are easy to understand.* If you stick to the language an eighth-grader would understand (and I am not referring to slang), you are in good shape.

2. *It must be conversational.* It is not an advertising theme or slogan; it is a conversational answer to the question, "What do you do?"

3. *It must create some attraction on the part of the other person.* It should make people want to talk with you, be with you, and learn from you.

4. *It must have a dream focus.* If it helps the prospect see the future as better than the present, you have a dream focus.

5. *It must contain the what and the who.* It defines outcomes and who would be served by working with you or buying from you.
6. *It must have a dual focus.* Create a two-part statement that has two outcomes and you will thereby appeal to a wider audience.

Here is my own defining statement that illustrates all of the above points:

I own a business that's designed to help our clients increase their sales and improve their management focus and effectiveness.

Take your time developing your defining statement. This one took me several hours over a period of a few weeks. But, once you have it, let it get a hold of you and believe it, memorize it, practice it, use it, and watch it galvanize the people with whom you interact.

Turn It Around
Know exactly what to say, regardless of the circumstances.

MISTAKE #57: *Selling Low Price Rather than High Value*

Most poorly trained salespeople tend to lower the price when they receive price resistance. The price will always seem high to a prospect or customer if the perceived value is low. The key to effectively handling price resistance is to understand this simple yet profound concept.

People say they want low price, but what they really want is low cost. What is the difference?

Price is what customers pay for your product or service *now*. Cost is what they pay for it *over time*. For example, they buy an inexpensive piece of equipment to save money now, but it is in constant need of repair because it breaks down frequently. They may have saved money initially, but their cost over time will be much higher than if they had invested more in a better piece of equipment.

In most cases, we get what we pay for. Buy cheap and you get less value and/or higher cost. Buy expensive and you get higher value and/or lower cost over time.

What are you selling: high value or low price? Personally, I would rather sell a high-priced product or service than a low-priced one. It is much easier to justify high price if the value is there, than poor quality and constant product or service problems.

Remember, the key to success in selling is building strong relationships. Poor quality at a low price, even though customers save money initially, is not in their best long-term interests. How do you want to be remembered by your customers—for low quality, or for a good value at a fair price?

Turn It Around
Create high perceived value so price is not an issue.

MISTAKE #58: *Selling Features and Not Customer Benefits*

Product or service features are what the product or service is. Product benefits are what the features do for the product. Customer benefits are what the features and product benefits do for the customer.

Prospects need to know what the features are, but they buy because of what those features do for them—that is, the customer benefits. Most salespeople sell features. A few of the better salespeople sell product benefits. The very successful salespeople sell customer benefits. What's the difference? Here is a simple presentation of all three.

"Mr. Prospect, one of the exceptional features of our product is that it is made of steel." (Feature.) "This gives the product durability." (Product benefit.) "What this means to you is that it will last a long time and require very little maintenance." (Customer benefit.)

Just giving the prospect a list of features may educate them on your service, but it won't get them to buy. Giving them the product benefits will help them understand the value of the service, but it won't get the sale closed. The key is to develop a presentation strategy that covers all three from the customer's point of view. There are two problems when it comes to a feature-based presentation:

1. Prospects will never picture themselves owning or using the service.
2. This approach makes it easier for them to use price as a reason not to buy.

I suggest you do two things regarding this part of the sales process:

1. Make a list of all of your features—yes, all of them.
2. Create a customer-focused benefit statement around each feature.

Turn It Around
Ensure that prospects understand what is in it for them.

MISTAKE #59: *Selling Everyone the Same*

A common mistake many salespeople make is that they sell to everyone in the same way. These salespeople fail to take into consideration that each buyer or prospect has very individual motives and reasons for what, when, and how they buy. One of the keys to effective selling is to sell the prospect the way they are comfortable buying, not the way you are comfortable selling. Let me explain further.

There are four major types of buyers: 1) those who want quick answers and the bottom line; 2) those who want lots of details, information, and accuracy; 3) those who want to create a relationship with you and get to know you; and 4) those who want to make buying a social event and want to have fun.

Each of these four types of buyers must be approached from their perspective and comfort zone. To give a ton of information on features and benefits to a prospect who wants only the bottom line will surely put you back on the street without a sale. To expect a fast decision—waltz in, give your presentation, and waltz out—with the relationship buyer will earn their contempt and distrust. The secret, and it really isn't a secret at all, is to have four—that's right, *four*—distinct selling styles, vocabularies, approaches, and presentations.

Your prospect will tell you what you need to tell them to sell them, but you must discover their buying style before you launch into your presentation. Not only must you present differently to the four, but you must also close them, service them, negotiate with them, and treat them uniquely. In one of my recent seminars, one of the participants came up to me during a break after we had discussed this idea and said, "I do all of this naturally." I hate to burst your illusion, but most of us tend to sell out of our own unique approach and not tailor our presentation to different buyers' styles.

Turn It Around
Customize your sales message and approach.

MISTAKE #60: *Not Relating to the Prospect*

If you have been in sales for more than six months, you have most likely heard from a manager or some other salesperson: "You have to start every presentation with some small talk. You have to break the ice, get to know them, or make them comfortable." Yes and no.

Some prospects want to get to know you, and you them. Others just want their problems solved or their needs and desires satisfied. Spending "getting to know you" time with prospects who do not want this is doomed to failure or at least lost momentum.

The key is to know how your prospect wants you to relate to them. I recommend that you begin every presentation with a simple question—whether you are selling Learjets or Tupperware.

"Ms. Prospect, I don't know how I and my organization can best be of service to you; the only way for me to determine that is if I can ask you a few questions. Is that okay?"

This approach does two very important things in the sales process:

1. It gives you control. The person who asks the questions controls the conversation. The person who talks the most dominates it. And in a sales situation you want to control it, not dominate it.
2. It gets the prospect talking and keeps them talking.

In my career I have discovered that poor prospects don't want a lot of questions; they just want you to get to the price. Good prospects want you to know what their needs, problems, circumstances, or wants are and if you can satisfy them.

You'll never know—and they will never know—if you do all of the talking.

Turn It Around
Always come from the prospect's perspective.

MISTAKE #61: *Seeing the Sale as a Transaction*

Poor salespeople focus on just closing the sale. Successful salespeople focus on creating relationships. Which is your approach?

Selling is not only about closing the current prospect on a particular product or service that solves one of their pressing problems, needs, or desires. It is also about building a trusting relationship and partnership with them by becoming a resource and helping them solve their ongoing problems, or satisfying their continuing and evolving needs and desires.

You must first evaluate your selling intent, the philosophy underlying the sales process, and how it impacts your ability to close this sale and the future relationship. If your focus is on the short-term versus the long-term, your intent is most likely only on moving products or services now. If your intent is to develop a long-term, mutually beneficial relationship with this new prospect, you may not sell this order, but that does not prevent you from beginning to build a positive relationship that can one day end in success. It takes more time, resources, and energy to generate a new customer than it does to keep an existing one. It is also easier to do more business with a present customer than it is to find more new ones.

What is your approach? Are you investing a greater proportion of your time and resources to continue to find new business, or to satisfy, develop, and keep existing business? I agree that a continual flow of new business is the lifeblood of growth and success in sales; however, don't underestimate the ability to use your present customers to help you with that mission.

Next, recognize that few customers will just give you their business. You must ask for it, but you also have to earn the right to get it. In my opinion, closing is more of a philosophy than a skill. It is more an attitude than a strategy. It is more about giving than getting, and it is more about service than your sales compensation.

Turn It Around
See the sale as part of an ongoing relationship.

MISTAKE #62: *Invalidating Prospects*

What is an invalidator? It is a person who puts other people down, insults them even subtly, disregards their opinions, does not listen, lets his own ego try to control other people, manipulates, or negates others' feelings. How do you know if you if you tend to invalidate people?

1. Do you interrupt prospects while they are talking?
2. Are you an active listener regardless of who is speaking or how?
3. Is your ego—the need to be right, look good—getting in your way?
4. Are you more concerned with your need to make the sale than with the prospect's needs?

What are the consequences of being an invalidator in sales? Let me give you a couple of illustrations that I witnessed in actual sales presentations:

1. At the end of a product presentation to UPS, the salesperson said, "Tell you what, I'll FedEx a

sample to you so you have it tomorrow to review." Dumb? Yes. Invalidation? Yes. How? Well, he sent the subtle signal that FedEx was more reliable than UPS to ship the sample. Now, whether he believed that really doesn't matter. He lost the sale.

2. While making a presentation to a Pepsi-Cola distributor, the prospect asked the salesperson if she would like something to drink. Before she realized what she had said, she blurted out, "Sure, I'd love a Coke." Dumb? Yes. Invalidation? Yes, for the same sort of reason as above.

There are hundreds of ways salespeople invalidate prospects every day. Ever say, "Let me repeat"? This assumes the prospect is hearing impaired, stupid, or inattentive.

Turn It Around
Treat prospects with respect and concern.

MISTAKE #63: *Not Listening*

Hearing and listening are two different things. Hearing is a physical act. Listening is a mental one. The ears collect sound waves and send them to the brain for interpretation. Just because you don't have a hearing problem doesn't necessarily mean you are a good listener.

One of the biggest complaints many prospects have about salespeople is that they don't listen. Why don't people listen?

1. They don't care about the other person.
2. They are more concerned with their own ideas or thoughts.
3. It takes too much work to listen, so they just fake it.
5. They don't know how to listen.
6. They think they are listening.
8. Their ego—the need to manipulate, control, or look good—gets in the way of their listening.
9. The other person's nonverbal communication style gets in the way.
10. They think they know more about the subject than the person who is talking.
11. They are preoccupied with their own stuff.

One of the greatest compliments you can pay a prospect or customer is to be willing to listen to them regardless of their speaking style, pace, education, or emotional circumstances.

Are you a good listener? One way to find out is to ask others to comment on your listening willingness and ability.

Turn It Around

Hang on the prospect's every word to ensure understanding.

MISTAKE #64: *Having a Poor Vocabulary*

The tools of the professional salesperson are words. We paint word pictures, we tell stories, we describe product or service features and benefits, we influence, we inspire, and we hope to convince people of the benefits of doing business with us. All of this requires a command of language. It amazes me how many salespeople have poor vocabularies. These people fail to realize that they are limiting their success, negatively impacting their destiny and lifestyle by not having the ability to use the right word at the right time in any communication situation.

The key is to have a good enough vocabulary to be able to communicate effectively with anyone, whether they have an outstanding vocabulary or a poor one. In both cases, we need to be able to use effective words that can be understood by our prospect or customer. The ability to articulate your feelings, attitudes, needs, skills, desires, and knowledge is one of the most important ingredients for success in sales and in life.

How is your vocabulary? Do you often find you overuse certain words because you lack the ability to use replacement words? Do you ever find yourself searching for just the right word for a particular situation? Is your vocabulary getting in the way of your future success? Do you tend to use—or overuse—profanity?

Here are a few ways to enlarge your vocabulary: crossword puzzles, Scrabble, magazines, or learning one new word a day (that's three hundred sixty-five new words a year). In five years, imagine what kind of a vocabulary you could have with that technique. When someone uses a word you are unfamiliar with, ask what it means. Get a daily calendar that gives you a new word each day, or try an audiobook on vocabulary improvement.

Turn It Around

Know the power of words and how they contribute to success.

MISTAKE #65: *Failing to Create a Sense of Urgency*

One of the critical factors in a successful sales outcome is the sense of urgency a prospect brings to the sales process. A question I have been asked many times in my sales seminars is: can you create a sense of urgency? Yes, but it takes skill, effective communication ability, that right attitude, product knowledge, and confidence.

What is a sense of urgency? Let's say you discover, for example, that your prospect's primary supplier is back-ordered and they needed the supplies yesterday.

Urgency means the prospect needs a solution, answer, product, or service *now*. Price is not the issue; detail is not the issue. Your ability to deliver according to their needs or expectations is the *only* issue. Why do many salespeople spend literally hours every week in front of prospects that have no sense of urgency? Yes, you have to spend some time with them to determine if there is a sense of urgency, but once you discover there isn't, or you can't create it, move on to the next prospect—the sooner the better.

How can you create a sense of urgency? By focusing on the critical business factors, weaknesses, problems, and needs, and showing the prospect how waiting will cost him more than he is going to want to pay. Let's look back at the above example. Assume that the current supplier is not back-ordered with the products your prospect needs. Here are a couple of questions to ask your prospect:

1. What would happen if your current supplier couldn't deliver?
2. Do you have a secondary source of supply should your current supplier let you down?

Turn It Around
Learn the prospect's dominant emotional buying motive.

CHAPTER 4

HANDLING OBJECTIONS AND CLOSING MISTAKES

Have you ever computed the cost of your lost sales revenue in a week or year?

My thirty-year research of the ratio of my clients' sales efforts to sales income—regardless of industry, organization size, individual sales experience, and market conditions—shows that the average salesperson has a one-to-five closing ratio on new prospects. If you are doing better than that, congratulations! If not, please read on.

Tens of thousands of ineffective sales calls are made every day by well-meaning but poorly trained salespeople. One of the common reasons why salespeople do not close more sales is the inability to effectively disarm sales resistance in advance or overcome sales objections during the sales process.

The extrapolated cost of lost revenue in a year from these lost sales is staggering, to say the least. I have developed a simple formula that helps you determine how much actual revenue you are losing or how much your sales group is losing in a year. I recommend you compute this number only if you are a hardy soul and on some kind of high blood pressure medicine.

1. Subtract the number of closed sales from the total number of presentations given to good prospects in a week by you or one of your average salespeople.

2. Now multiply the remaining number (lost sales) by your average sales income per closed customer. Granted, this number will vary, but it will give you a good indicator. If you don't know the average income per customer, determine that

first. This will give you the lost total revenue for you or an average sales rep in a week.

3. If you are a sales manager or executive: multiply that number by the total number of sales reps in your sales force. This will give you the total lost revenue for the week by your combined sales group.

4. Now multiply this number by fifty-two. Bingo, you've got the magic number of your lost revenue or the lost revenue of your sales team in a year.

Here is an example for a typical rep:

- Twelve appointments per week: three sales, nine no-sales
- Average income per sale: $1,000
- Lost revenue by this rep in one week: $9,000
- As a manager, if you have ten reps, that's $90,000 in lost revenue in one week
- Times fifty-two weeks: that's $4,680,000 in lost revenue in one year

We only used $1,000 for an average sale. You can imagine what the number would be if your average sale was much higher!

I understand that:

- every product and service has a different sales cycle
- every product and service has more or less competition
- every organization has more or less corporate resources required for support and sales costs
- every sales rep has a unique territory
- every sales rep has a different level of competence

But the point remains: even if you used better-than-average numbers and favorable sales conditions, I guarantee your revenues per week and per year or the revenues of your salespeople could be much, *much* higher.

Learning to handle sales resistance effectively is one of the best ways to improve your sales results. Naturally, it is important to try to close a good prospect rather than a poor one, but we have covered the prospecting and qualification issue in a previous chapter.

Keep in mind that the frequency, number, and type of sales objections are excellent clues that will help you determine whether you have a good prospect or a bad one.

MISTAKE #66: *Not Disarming Objections Early*

There are only two ways to handle sales resistance: answer objections when they come up or disarm them in advance. Which do you think is the most effective approach? Traditional sales training for many years has suggested that salespeople should develop a number of pat answers to common sales objections and then, when these objections surface, give the memorized response. Although this strategy may be effective from time to time, there is a much better method for handling these potential sales busters: disarm.

In order to disarm sales objections, you need to know what they are before they become your prospect's focal point. A dumb approach is to give your presentation to your prospect while these sales questions, objections, problems—whatever you want to call them—are hiding beneath the surface, all the while preventing your prospect from listening to your message in an unbiased way.

If they are going to come up, it is better to get them out earlier rather than later. The way to do this is to ask simple questions early in the sales process before your appointment, early in the questioning stage, or on the telephone while asking general qualifying questions.

Here are a couple of questions to consider:

1. What would be your main reason for us not doing business together?
2. If there is one thing that would prevent you from participating in this program, what would that be?

Turn It Around
Discover potential sales resistance early.

MISTAKE #67: *Seeing Price Objections as a Problem*

Prospects and customers want several things from their suppliers: fair price, quality products and services, and timely service. Consumer surveys say that most consumers want timely and responsive service first, quality products and services second, and low price third. It is vital to understand the difference between price, cost, and perceived value. Price is what people pay for what they buy. Cost is what they pay for what they buy over time; in other words, the cost of doing it late, wrong, or not at all. Perceived value is what they want for the money they are paying.

Most consumers tell salespeople that what they want is low price, when what they really want is low cost. Now I know that many of you will take issue with this statement, but I only ask that you consider for a moment what you as a consumer want. Do you want the cheapest product, or the product that solves your problem and answers your need or desire?

People object to price when they feel that what you are asking them to pay is higher than their perceived value. Most poor salespeople, when they encounter price resistance, lower the price. Most of the time, it is not a price or cost issue, but one of too little perceived value by the prospect.

The real sales professionals focus on value—what the product or service does for the customer—and not price. They understand that price is an issue, but not the most important one. Price will always seem high when perceived value is low. It should therefore be obvious that you never want to introduce price too soon in the sales process—not until you have had the opportunity to build value in the prospect's mind. If you have a price-only buyer (they are out there), you must decide if that business is worth it to you in the long run.

Turn It Around
Never accept price as the primary objection.

MISTAKE #68: *Fearing Sales Objections*

Objections by good prospects are not negative. They are a sign of interest, a buying signal, or a request for more information. Objections from poor prospects are their strategy for getting rid of you.

I would like you to think of sales objections as unanswered questions rather than sales resistance. In other words, what is the prospect really asking when they say things like:

- "The price is too high." Could they be asking, "Why should I pay this much?"

- "I am happy with our current supplier or vendor." Could they be asking, "What are the advantages of switching to your organization or your product or service?"

- "We are going to purchase this product from you, but we need to wait until the end of the month, next quarter, or next year." Could they be asking, "What are the advantages or benefits of doing this now rather than later?"

- "We need to check with some other suppliers before we make our decision." Could they be asking, "How is your service or product better than your competitors?"

- "We really don't need this product." Could they be asking, "What problem does it solve? What pain does it ease?"

Turn It Around
Develop proven techniques for answering objections.

MISTAKE #69: *Projecting Your Personal Biases*

The objection that you will tend to have the most difficulty answering successfully is the one that is most consistent with your own value system. What do I mean by this?

If you are a price buyer, and your prospect objects to price, you will tend to accept their objection. If you are the type of buyer who tends to think decisions over before making a purchase and your prospect says to you, "We need to think this over," you will tend to go along with their objection as rational or making perfect sense because that is the way you buy.

This simple act of accepting sales objections that resonate with you because you can relate to them is nothing more than projecting your personal attitudes into the sales process. You don't have the right to do this. Furthermore, it makes no sense to assume that just because a prospect says that the price is too high, they actually believe it or mean it.

People often don't know what they want or why. People often buy things that they don't need. People sometimes lie about what they want or why they buy. Why? Who knows—they just do.

When you project your personal biases onto the sales process, you are assuming that everyone who buys, buys like you and for the same reasons. You are also assuming that when they don't buy for a reason that is similar to one of your reasons, it makes perfect sense.

This attitude sooner or later is going to cost you a lot of sales.

Turn It Around
Stay neutral during the sales process.

MISTAKE #70: *Not Asking for the Business*

A number of years ago, *Sales and Marketing* magazine did a survey. Their research indicated that 60 percent of the time in a sales-closing situation, the salesperson failed to ask for the order.

People want to buy things, but often they don't want to make the decision to buy things. Why? They want a better life, a more successful business, or happier relationships, but they don't want to commit the money, time, or energy that will give them these things.

Consider this: during every sales presentation, a sale is closed. Either you sell your product or service to the prospect or they sell you on why they don't need it, can't afford it, or don't need it now.

Why don't salespeople—after going through all the time, energy, and effort to present their product or service—ask for the business?

I have discovered that there are five main reasons:

1. They fear a "no" or rejection.
2. They feel that if they have done a good job presenting the product or service, the prospect will buy.

3. They don't know how to close the sale.
4. They don't have a closing strategy.
5. They never got control of the sales process from the beginning and they don't know how to get it at the end.

Turn It Around

Ask for the order.

MISTAKE #71: *Lacking a Closing Strategy*

Closing the sale is not an event. It is:

- having effective prospecting skills
- having a closing awareness or attitude
- related to everything that you have done up to the final close
- based on the ability to come from the customer's perspective
- grounded in the ability to create a high level of trust

Attempting to close a sale without all of the above criteria is to invite a "no sale" result. Most poor prospects attempt to get the salesperson to move to the close quickly and then base their decision not to buy on price or some other stall tactic that most salespeople can't effectively handle. Therefore, the entire sales process comes down to a nickel or some differential that you can't control.

Few salespeople have a "closing strategy"—a process that they follow with each and every sales opportunity. They ask a few questions, jump into the presentation too soon, try to overcome any objections, and go for the close. The successful salespeople know the outcome long before they get to the end of this routine process, and they do it by ensuring that each of the above steps is in place before they ask their closing question.

People generally don't like to make buying decisions. The primary reason is that they don't want to make a poor or wrong decision. For years, traditional sales closing methods asked people to make a decision. For example: Do you want it in green or red? (Alternative choice close.) Do you want to use your pen or mine? (Action close.) Can we write up an order now? (Direct close.)

Each of these closing techniques, even though it can work, has two fundamental problems:

1. It asks the prospect to make a decision.
2. The average salesperson is uncomfortable using it.

Since people don't like to make decisions, I suggest you stop asking them to. Here is a simple close that I have been using for over thirty years: make the buying decision for the prospect, and ask them to agree with the decision you have made. It goes like this: "Let's do this, is that okay?" "Let's arrange for delivery on the fifteenth, is that okay?" "Let's get together on Thursday at 10 a.m., is that okay?"

This close works for three reasons:

1. It gets a decision made, but the prospect doesn't feel as though they have to make it. By agreeing with you, they, in essence, do make the decision. I have found that people want to get decisions made, but don't want to make them.
2. It is common language. I guarantee in the next two to three days you will either say to someone or hear from someone, "Let's go to the movie, okay?" or "Let's go out to dinner tonight, okay?"
3. It is easy to remember and use, and it gets the job done.

When you use this close, the prospect has only three options:

1. They can go along with both your decision for them and your recommendation.
2. They go along with your decision, but don't like your recommendation. In both cases, you have a close.
3. They go along with neither your decision nor recommendation. No sale. However, using this with a qualified prospect gives you a 2-out-of-3 closing percentage.

If two people want to do business together, they won't let the details get in the way. If they don't want to do business, any detail will get in the way.

Turn It Around
Have a closing methodology that works and is repeatable.

MISTAKE #72: *Advertising Concessions*

Advertising your willingness to make a concession before you are asked to make one is insanity. What do I mean by this?

During the presentation, you make the statement that you can give the prospect a discount. They haven't asked for a discount. They may not need a discount, but what have you now set up by making that statement? They are going to ask for a discount unless, of course, they are deaf. And then you act surprised!

How about this one:

Your price list says something like: "Suggested retail price." Now I ask you, are you going to be surprised when the prospect asks for a price concession at the end of the sales presentation?

Every day millions of salespeople make offhand remarks or casual statements that send the message to the prospect—loud and clear—that this price, these terms or this feature is a negotiable item.

I urge you to carefully evaluate all of the statements you make while selling to see if you are advertising your willingness to make a concession later in the process. One way to do this is to look at your most frequent negotiating requests from prospects to see if there is anything you have done or said that may have set this in motion.

Turn It Around
Address concessions only when asked.

MISTAKE #73: *Lacking a Lost-Sale Strategy*

As I mentioned earlier, even the best salespeople can lose business: sales are not closed, customers decide to use a new supplier, businesses no longer need our products or services, or any number of other valid reasons. You cannot sell to everyone and you cannot keep customers for life. It is a myth, no matter what you may have heard or read. The key is not to lose them because of poor performance, poor quality, poor service, or poor sales skills.

Regardless of the reason behind lost business, knowing how to handle such episodes will be a key factor in your success. Here are a few suggestions to use when you lose a sale:

1. Thank them for their time by following up with a thank-you note or letter.
2. Follow up with an after-sales critique or evaluation.
3. Follow up with additional sources of proof—testimonials, articles, etc.
4. Accept the fact that things, people, and businesses change.

5. Find out what your competitor did better than you to get the business.
6. Don't let it negatively affect your attitude. Keep at it.

Remember: Staying power over the long haul is much more beneficial than quick short-term success.

Turn It Around
Know how to save lost sales before they are lost.

MISTAKE #74: *Lacking Walk-Away Power*

Sooner or later, you will have to walk away from a prospect or a client relationship that is no longer worth your time, energy, corporate resources, or willingness to continue. What are the characteristics that could contribute to this decision? Here are a few to think about:

1. The potential for additional business just isn't there.
2. The time, energy, or corporate resources to keep this sale or relationship active is no longer a wise investment.
3. You have lost control of the sales process.
4. Your intuition tells you to walk away from this one.
5. The prospect or client's only interest is price, and they are not concerned about service, quality, or your ability to help them solve problems or grow their business.

There are other reasons, but most will fall into the above five categories. Here are a few questions to consider:

1. Are you failing to walk away from any business that you feel you should?
2. Do you have inconsistent reasons for not walking away from some business?
3. Do you have a walk-away philosophy or strategy?
4. Do you have a successful sales strategy that you use consistently to keep the sales process alive when the prospect or client forces you into what feels like a walk-away position?

I am not advising giving up too soon, not using creative sales appeals, or terminating the sales process because you may be over your head. I am, however, suggesting that you have a walk-away philosophy and strategy that you can use as a template when the value of current business or potential business is in question.

Turn It Around
Know when a prospect is not a prospect and walk away.

MISTAKE #75: *Negotiating When You Should Be Selling*

Effective negotiating is not a substitute for effective selling skills. Many salespeople believe that they need to be better negotiators, when what they really need is improved sales skills. Let's define the requirements for effective and successful selling:

1. Maintaining a positive outlook and an enthusiastic and passionate demeanor
2. Finding and identifying good prospects (those who have a need, desire, and sense of urgency for a solution to a problem that your product or service will give them)
3. Positioning your product or service in the mind of the prospect as the best possible solution for their available resources
4. Presenting the characteristics (features and customer benefits) of your product or service to the prospect in such a way that they easily see how these solutions will be achieved
5. Disarming any unspoken sales objections during this process and then asking for the business

6. Servicing your clients to ensure repeat and referral business, as well as customer satisfaction
7. Maintaining effective and accurate sales records

Let's define negotiating. Negotiating begins where selling leaves off. It is finding those areas between the customer and the salesperson where there are differences or a need for compromise in these areas:

1. Features—what they can or cannot live without
2. Delivery terms—what they need and what you can give them
3. Financial terms—again, what they need and what you can allow

Negotiating is finding a way to reach a meeting point or common ground where you and your prospect can agree with each other's circumstances and still have a win-win relationship.

Turn It Around
Know when to sell and when to negotiate.

CHAPTER 5

TIME AND TERRITORY MANAGEMENT MISTAKES

You can't manage time. Time passes.

You can't use time in advance, store it up, use it twice, save it, use it again, speed it up, slow it down, or do anything with it. All you can do in a framework of passing time is manage people, activities, attitudes, resources, decisions, problems, failures, successes, risks, money, and circumstances.

If you think you have a time-management problem, I would ask you another question. What, from the previous list, are you having a problem managing? Time management is a misnomer.

Salespeople who seem to get more done don't do it with more or less time. Each of us gets twenty-four hours a day, 168 hours a week, 672 hours a month, and 8,064 hours a year to work, play, learn, grow, travel, sleep, eat, and engage in any number of other activities.

Why is it that some salespeople achieve more results than other people? They don't have more time, but what they do have is better personal management skills. They are better organized, more focused, or more effective using the time they have. They have priorities, and they keep focused on them—whether it is spending time with grandchildren or putting together million-dollar deals.

I love to work, but I also want to have a life other than my work. With organization, commitment, and focus, anything is possible.

How are you doing? Do you have enough time for everything in your life that is important? Is any area of your life getting short-changed?

A simple task to determine where you are wasting time or not using your time effectively is to keep a record of how you use your time in hour blocks for a week. I guarantee if you do this, you will quickly determine where you need some schedule, activity, or priority modification.

MISTAKE #76: *Not Using Your Time Wisely*

For the past several years, I have been surveying my sales audiences to determine how much time salespeople actually spend selling. Let me define what I mean by selling: the amount of time you spend in front of a prospect or customer or on the telephone selling them. This does not include:

- Travel time
- Meetings
- After-sales service
- Waiting time
- Problem solving
- Administrative responsibilities

I realize that all of the above are important and often required by either your boss or your client or prospect, and that they can indirectly contribute to satisfying a customer relationship, repeat business, and customer loyalty. Having said that, how much time do you think the typical salesperson spends selling (and that's what you get paid to do)? Eighty percent? Fifty percent? Thirty percent?

You may be surprised to find out (and please keep in mind that my research is very unscientific, but fairly consistent) that the actual amount of time salespeople spend selling averages 10–20 percent of their total work time! Now consider if you will: what you are currently earning is based on spending less than 30 percent of your time (on the average) selling. Imagine what could happen to your income if you could increase that to 50 percent? You would still be spending less than 60 percent of your time selling. Could you increase your income by at least 10 percent? I'll bet you could, easily.

Turn It Around
Use your sales time wisely by planning everything.

MISTAKE #77: *Using Technology as a Crutch*

Many salespeople rely too heavily on technology as a sales tool to:

- Contact new prospects
- Maintain contact with current customers
- Handle after-sales service issues
- Cultivate relationships with customers

Technology is a wonderful tool and has made it possible for salespeople to save time and stay in touch—but at what cost? Relationships, especially sales relationships, are about people. People want and need human contact. An email tip is a wonderful way to stay in touch with my clients and prospects, but it will never replace a personal visit or telephone call.

How often have you sent an email rather than picking up the phone?

How often have you sent a fax instead of setting an appointment with a customer to discuss the issue?

Yes, technology often lets you get more done, easier and faster. (I mean, I am sitting at my computer in my home office with a glass of wine while I write this, and who knows where you are or what you will be doing when you read this.) I love technology, but I also enjoy talking with my friends, visiting with clients, and getting to know people on a personal basis, face to face. Nothing can ever replace that—not the fastest computer, glitziest website, or smallest hand-held device.

Be careful not to assume that everyone is as technologically advanced or competent as you are.

Turn It Around
Don't let technology replace the human touch.

MISTAKE #78: *Losing Focus*

An ongoing challenge for many salespeople is the ability to stay focused in the midst of personal turmoil.

Salespeople who cannot separate their personal life challenges from their career responsibilities generally find that their problems resonate in some nonverbal or emotional way.

When you cannot separate these personal issues from your career roles, you will tend to:

1. Reduce your positive state of mind, therefore impacting your success
2. Increase stress that will impact your health and ability to be creative
3. Send mixed messages to your prospect or customer
4. Lose the competitive edge
5. Negatively impact the ability to listen effectively and communicate with integrity

Here are a few steps to consider in order to separate the areas of your life. Do this so that one area will not have more control over another area than you choose to give it.

1. Focus on something positive rather than negative in the area of your life that concerns you.
2. Spend time before each call or appointment in a relaxation or short meditation period.
3. Focus on your long-term life goals and your progress when life throws you a curve.
4. Develop little routines or positive anchors for when you are troubled.
5. Carry some personal physical reminder with you of what is positive in your life.

Turn It Around

Learn to compartmentalize your personal life and career.

MISTAKE #79: *Not Being Prepared to Sell*

Selling today is easier in many ways, but it is also more difficult in other ways.

It is easier because of the Internet, globalization, improved customer education and sophistication, better quality products and services, improved organizational management, and increased selling-skills training.

It is more difficult because of the Internet, globalization, improved customer education and sophistication, increased consumer choices, organizational downsizing and restructuring, reduced layers of decision makers, time compression, organization turnover, and product life cycles.

So, how is the salesperson of today supposed to survive, succeed, or even excel? There are a number of actions that can and should be undertaken:

1. Develop positive sales rituals.
2. Develop emotional and psychological anchors that keep you focused.
3. Read some self-help material every day.

4. Study the competition.
5. Know your own products and services better than anyone.
6. Develop career advocates.
7. Become a positive resource for your prospects and clients.
8. Keep asking yourself, "How can I do it better?"
9. Network with people who can help you.
10. Develop strategic alliances in your career with people who can advance your career success.
11. Subscribe to and read publications that service your industry or the industries of your clients and prospects.
12. Think ahead of your client, not just along with them.

Turn It Around

Start. Act. Follow through.

MISTAKE #80: *Poor Sales Forecasting*

One of the things management expects of salespeople is bottom-up feedback in the area of sales forecasting. Unfortunately, many sales managers shove their sales forecasts down the throats of their sales staff due to the demands and expectations for sales increases from senior management.

Salespeople are better equipped to forecast future sales results in their territory if they are in touch with their customers' and prospects' needs, problems, budgets, changes, and competitive initiatives. In order to come up with numbers that are reflective of "the real world" and satisfy the demands of management, salespeople must understand the factors that impact their future sales results. Some of these are:

1. Present sales levels per customer or prospect
2. Future needs, concerns, and desires of customers and prospects
3. Competitive activities in the sales territory
4. General market conditions
5. Quality of the relationship with their customers
6. New or future product or service opportunities

7. Whether the territory has potential or is a maintenance territory

There are many others, but these tend to determine the accuracy of any sales forecast, whether weekly, monthly, or yearly. The key premises to remember when forecasting are:

1. People buy when they are ready to buy—not when you need to sell.
2. Ignoring competitors' initiatives will ensure a lack of integrity in your results.
3. You can't make up for poor sales skills with extra effort or time.
4. Numbers pulled out of the air will haunt you later.

Turn It Around
Blend optimism with reality when forecasting.

MISTAKE #81: *Poor Territory Management*

Many salespeople will waste a great deal of time calling on poor prospects, trying to turn poor prospects into customers, or trying to close prospects that do not want or need what they are selling. One of the key characteristics in more effective territory management is doing a better job of qualifying prospects prior to giving them your time, energy, or corporate resources. Let's look at a few ways to better manage your time and territory management.

1. Ask more effective questions earlier in the sales process.
2. Pay attention to answers to determine whether this is a good time to sell to this prospect.
3. Develop a customer profile to use as a template for your prospecting.
4. Spend more prospecting time getting referrals.
5. Develop strategic alliances to help you improve your prospecting results.
6. Plan your call activities early in the day, week, or month.

7. Don't give poor prospects more time than they deserve.

8. Develop a daily checklist of what you will need to be effective.

9. Get more of your prospects to visit your location, plant, or office.

10. Don't spend time giving presentations to non-decision makers.

Turn It Around

See your territory as an abundant source of business.

MISTAKE #82: *Spending Too Much Time on Poor Prospects*

It is impossible to sell every possible prospect. Poor salespeople have the philosophy, "If they will see me, I will see them." Successful salespeople know that some prospects are better prospects than others. They also know that every customer is also a prospect for additional business or referrals. They use a customer profile as a template for determining who is worthy of their time. They use this system to determine who is the best-qualified prospect for them to see now.

Poor salespeople try to turn poor prospects into customers. The pros don't have time for this kind of activity. They want to spend their limited selling time with only well-qualified prospects.

How do you know if you are wasting time on poor prospects? Ask yourself:

1. Is the sales process taking longer than usual with this prospect?
2. Do they tend to give me the run-around?
3. Is there no sense of urgency with this prospect?

4. Do they fail to return calls or respond to my initiatives?
5. Am I applying too much pressure to get this sale closed?
6. Does this prospect trust me?
7. Do I know their dominant emotional buying motives?
8. Am I trying to make my timetable their timetable?

There are only two reasons to spend time, resources, and energy on poor prospects:

1. You have nothing else to do.
2. You are failing.

And neither of these will contribute to increased sales or success.

Turn It Around
Use a prospect profile to decide who is worthy of your time.

CHAPTER 6

RECORD-KEEPING MISTAKES

Have you ever experienced a sales slump? Or just not achieved the results that you believed you should have? If you have been selling for at least two or three years, I guarantee you have had some tough months, or even a challenging sales year.

Success in selling requires many skills, attitudes, abilities, and personal values. When a salesperson experiences a down cycle in their success, it is impossible to look at just one single area of their approach to the sales process or their attitudes at any given time in order to determine where the cause of the problem is. For example, if you are having trouble closing sales, is it because you have poor closing skills or could it be that you are trying to close poor prospects? If you are having trouble getting through to the key economic buyer or decision-maker, is it because you don't know who they are or could it be that your low self-esteem prevents you from feeling confident or comfortable even calling on prospects at this level?

Determining where the problem is requires information—lots of accurate information about sales ratios, actual numbers, trends, and comparisons. It is difficult to take corrective action if you are not aware of the cause of your problem or the actions to take. Just working harder, longer hours, or continuing to repeat the same behaviors over and over again is not the answer. This approach will not solve your problem, but it will keep you busy.

Many sales organizations and managers require regular call reports from their salespeople, but those reports are, in most cases, just sales busywork. They provide little, if any, value for the salesperson or the sales manager on where current or potential sales problems are or their causes. One of the many common denominators among top salespeople is their ruthless evaluation of activities, behaviors, results, and progress or lack of progress toward their goals. Most poor salespeople will tell you they don't have the time to keep complete and accurate sales activity and results records.

MISTAKE #83: *Not Keeping Records*

Keeping accurate sales records does not have to be a time-consuming or difficult task. All that is necessary is that you develop the discipline and form the habits necessary to ensure that you are always working from a position of knowledge and understanding and not one of ignorance and uncertainty. There are a variety of activities and results that you might want to consider tracking to ensure you know what is working and what isn't. Here are just a few of the items I recommend that you track each day, week, month, or year:

1. Your average sales volume or revenue per prospect
2. Your average amount of time from first contact to closed sale
3. The top five reasons why prospects don't buy from you
4. The average number of calls and appointments to close a sale
5. The average number of referrals from clients
6. The percentage of appointments to closed sales

7. The number of new prospects in your sales funnel each week or month
8. The percentage of time spent selling versus after-sales service or administrative tasks
9. The average number of new prospect presentations given per day, week, or month
10. Your average number of sales per week, month, and year
11. The average number of lost sales each week, month, and year

Turn It Around

Spend time every day writing down vital sales facts.

MISTAKE #84: *Not Evaluating Your Results*

Okay, so now you have created routine record-keeping activities each day, week, month, and year. If you will devote just five minutes a day; thirty minutes a week; one hour a month; and a day at the end of each year, this time—if well spent—will guarantee that you are in touch with the reality of the relationship between your activities and results. I recommend you purchase two of my sales tools to give you more in-depth information on this subject: the book *Soft Sell* and the yearly planning manual *The Sales Success Planner*.

Once you have the records, it is critical that you evaluate them honestly to determine where you need to make adjustments or modifications in your behavior, attitudes, or skills.

The vital statistics you are looking for are the ratios derived from the records you have maintained.

Here are a few examples. What is your ratio between:

- Sales to new customers and to repeat buyers?
- Prospecting telephone calls and appointments?

- Sales presentations and closed sales?
- Sales to referrals versus cold calling or other methods of prospecting?

Now it's just a matter of asking yourself some hard questions, such as:

- Why did your sales average increase or decrease in a week or month?
- Why did you lose more sales in one period versus another?
- Why is time to close the sales cycle increasing?

Turn It Around
Evaluate your results weekly in order to plot better methods.

MISTAKE #85: *Not Establishing Benchmarks*

There is one way to ensure success in sales in the future: reduce or eliminate the number of mistakes, poor decisions, and failures. Keep in mind that each of these can be very positive for the person who routinely examines their life decisions and actions. The problem is, most people don't.

The vast majority of salespeople just truck along not connecting today's challenges with yesterday's poor judgment, choices, or actions. Establish benchmarks in your life to guide you toward your goals. Benchmarks can give you a number of critical advantages as you move from one day to the next. Some of them are:

1. Accountability
2. Recommitment
3. Reevaluation
4. Proper direction
5. A measuring device
6. Renewed belief
7. Growing passion
8. A warning sign

A benchmark can be analogous to the road signs you see while making the long drive to a vacation in an area you have never been to before. It can also be a warning signal that something is amiss. If you are not careful, you may never make it to your destination. Here are a few benchmarks to consider:

1. What are you going to do better this year to accelerate your progress?
2. What guidelines do you have in place to ensure you are heading in the right direction?
3. What records do you need to keep to ensure that you stay on track?
4. To whom can you give permission to hold you accountable?
5. Are you going to spend regular programmed time in reflection and reevaluation?

I believe that regularly measuring activity to learn which activities generate the greatest degree of success with the least amount of pain and stress is one of the best ways to ensure that the time and effort you put into your career, business, or life will yield outstanding positive outcomes.

*"What we do not understand,
we do not possess."*

—GOETHE

Turn It Around

Create guidelines as standards to measure your success.

MISTAKE #86: *Failing to Improve Every Day*

Selling is getting more competitive every minute.

- There are more suppliers, offering more choices.
- There are more ways to purchase.
- There are higher consumer expectations.
- There is less consumer loyalty.
- There is increased difficulty getting to decision makers.
- There is more pressure from management to sell more at higher margins.
- There is technology that is driving everything faster and faster.
- There is more information available today about customers, competitors, and the marketplace than at any time in history.

So, what is today's professional salesperson to do? Quit? Hide? Play more golf? Jump ship to another industry, firm, or territory? Many have tried all of the above, but soon learned that they can't hide from the relentless advance of their lives, businesses, and the world. There is one thing you can and must do if you hope to survive, succeed, and prosper in this new world order—spend increasing amounts of regular time and energy on learning for self-improvement. And not just more, but what is necessary for success, peace, balance, and lifestyle.

How much time do you spend in regular planned and focused learning? If it is not a priority in your life, you will soon discover that your competitors are stealing your business before you even know it. Don't risk it. Start today: reading, listening, attending seminars, and investing in yourself. I guarantee that over the next few years it will pay off more than you ever dreamed possible.

Turn It Around
Spend time every day improving your skills and attitudes.

CHAPTER 7

AFTER-SALES SERVICE MISTAKES

The mission for many of today's organizations is improved customer satisfaction and retention through better after-sales service.

There are many companies that have put real teeth and accountability into their employee training to ensure they get the consistent results they say they desire. Unfortunately, there are many more companies who have only given lip service to this customer-driven philosophy or approach.

In this chapter, I will share with you what I believe are the Twelve Laws of Effective After-Sales Service. These concepts must be integrated into any sales culture, corporate philosophy, or program to ensure integrity between policies and procedures on one hand and customer perceptions and attitudes on the other.

Effective after-sales service is not a slogan, advertising program, button that everyone wears, or banner touting a "we care" attitude. It is a mindset or attitude that penetrates every department of the organization. It is a philosophy that is understood and embraced by every employee, regardless of position, length of service, or responsibilities. It is consistent, regardless of the point in the week or month, market pressures, department or branch, current sales results, current cash flow, management philosophy of the day, or market position.

It is not a "program" that is funded for the short term, but a corporate lifestyle that is ongoing, regardless of the whims of management, the fickleness of customers, or the dynamics of the marketplace.

What prevents an organization from building this consciousness into the fabric of its management team and employees?

1. If the corporate culture has been traditionally profit- or earnings-driven, then it will be difficult to shift gears to a customer-driven philosophy.

2. If communication is heavily weighted in a top-down direction, you can bet that it will take lots of time and follow-through to refocus to a bottom-up style.

3. If the management style is closed, authoritative, or hierarchical, upper management will—unless totally and completely committed to changing the attitudes of the organization as a whole—generally abandon this new and challenging change in philosophy sooner or later.

4. If employees have too much on their plate, because your business style is to run "lean and mean," it will be difficult to consistently enforce the policies and procedures necessary to maintain the integrity of actions consistent with your stated objective of satisfied customers.

An effective after-sales service philosophy requires constant vigilance and dedication to see it through, regardless of how difficult it may be to maintain the integrity of those policies and procedures that directly or indirectly impact your customers and their expectations of your product or service and organization performance. One way to determine the effectiveness of your after-sales service philosophy is to regularly solicit customer feedback in a variety of ways.

Now for the key to effective after-sales service:

The Twelve Laws of Effective After-Sales Service

Law #1: The customer is not always right.
However, the goal is not to discredit, embarrass, belittle, or challenge them in a destructive way. What we need to do is discover the source or cause of their incorrect perceptions, beliefs, or attitudes. The next step is to determine if the organization has contributed significantly to these incorrect feelings or if their source is the competition, the marketplace, or their Uncle Harry.

Law #2: The customer is never completely wrong.
There is always some element of their perception

that is a true reflection of reality as they see it. The customer can be a teacher for us if we will keep an open mind and receptive, neutral demeanor. They can mirror back to us where our advertising, distribution methods, pricing strategies, administrative policies, or marketing or sales methods need improvement, refinement, or a major overhaul.

Law #3: The customer deserves your best, regardless of the time of day, day of the week, or month of the year.

The fact that you worked late last night because it was your monthly inventory or your annual sales blowout should not become the customer's problem. The fact that you just returned from a week on the road working trade shows is not the customer's concern.

Law #4: The customer deserves your best regardless of your training, length of service, or any other prevailing corporate attitude.

So you are sixty days away from retirement and just filling time, waiting to get behind the wheel of your RV. Or you are a brand new sales rep whining that manufacturing just doesn't understand. Or you are on the first week of the job and still can't master this new piece of equipment. Or you are overstocked on a particular item, so you cut back on stocking the items that your customer uses regularly and ask if he will accept a substitute. These circumstances and thousands of others like them, if they become the customer's problem, will cause him to seek out your competitor.

Law #5: Don't pass the buck.

Whoever hears about a problem owns the problem. How often have you been transferred several times before you finally got to the right person? Have you ever heard, "It's not my job, problem, or function"? Don't get defensive or upset when a customer brings you a concern or complaint. Accept the fact that the problem exists and help get it solved.

Law #6: Don't be too busy for your customers and don't make it difficult for them to do business with you.

How many times have you as a customer gotten the feeling that you are an interruption in an employee's day or workload? Have you as a customer ever been made to feel like you shouldn't be having a problem with a product or service, that it is your fault that the item broke? Don't treat your customers this way.

Law #7: Employees are customers too.

Every employee that ever does anything within an organization is ultimately doing it indirectly for the customer. That makes every employee an ambassador, spokesperson, or representative of the customer. When an employee fails to serve another employee in an effective or timely manner, sooner or later the customer will feel the repercussions.

Law #8: If you must use technology, make it user-friendly.

Within the past week, I have had five voice mail systems hang up on me. When I called back to get a person, I had to spend several minutes of my valuable time wading through endless recorded dribble. I finally called another supplier.

Law #9: Say what you will do and do what you say you will.

Follow through, keep your promises, honor your commitments, and keep your customer informed of your progress. Customers will tend to be more understanding, patient, and tolerant if you communicate with them with integrity and in a timely manner.

Law #10: Be interested, care, and act like you are glad the customer is doing business with you.

People like doing business with people who appreciate their business. People are willing to give more of their business and money to businesses that are friendly, accommodating, and interested. You show you care by having up-to-date product knowledge; knowing who does what in your organization so you don't have to keep a client on hold for ten minutes, while you try to find someone to solve her problem; and smiling, even if it hurts.

Law #11: Keep private things private.

If I am a client, I am not interested in your personal problems or corporate politics. I do not have the time to listen to who did what to whom and why in your organization, nor am I interested. I don't want to know that you are looking for another job. Sharing private, confidential, or personal information—whether you are the CEO or receptionist—is in poor taste and unprofessional. It also makes me wonder how much of my business you share with other customers or suppliers.

Law #12: Think ahead of the customer with a problem-solving attitude.

To survive and prosper in this decade and this new century will require that organizations and their employees think well ahead of their customers and their potential future desires, problems, and needs. It will be too late if you just wait for the customer to bring their problems to you or communicate to you their future desires or needs.

MISTAKE #87: *Lacking an Effective Follow-Up Process*

One of the techniques used to improve client relationships and sales results is to have an effective follow-up system or strategy for prospects and customers. An effective follow-up can be a telephone call, fax, email, letter, hand-written note, personal visit, or any combination of these.

The advantages of follow-up (and the disadvantages of not following up) should be obvious, but for those of you who are not sure, here are a few:

1. Remember: if you are out of sight, you are out of mind.
2. It sends the message that you are a professional.
3. It implies that you are in it (sales, the relationship) not just for the money.
4. It helps competitor-proof the business.
5. It makes you look better than your competitor.

So, when are some times to follow up, and how should you do it? Here are just a few ways:

1. After a client or prospect visit: thank them for their time.
2. After you have closed a sale: thank them for the business.
3. After you have solved a problem for them: ensure that they are satisfied.
4. After you have received a referral from them: thank them for it.
5. After you have made a commitment to them: follow through with it to show you meant it.
6. Follow up after meeting them at a trade show.
7. Follow up after sending them sales material.
8. Follow up after receiving an inquiry.
9. Follow up after sending them to your website to do some research.

In summary, here are two general rules for when to follow up:

1. After they have done anything for you
2. After you have done anything for them

Turn It Around

When in doubt, follow up.

MISTAKE #88: *Not Watching Trends*

Are you watching the trends so you can keep your customers informed about how business and economic trends may impact their business in the future? What are some of the types of trends you should be observing?

- Economic trends
- Market trends
- Technology trends
- Buyer perceptions
- Product evolution
- Service needs and expectations
- Buyer groups

I can tell you that over 75 percent of my business today and for the past twenty-five years has come from only five major industries—and I selected those industries in 1973. Was it luck? I am not that lucky. Was it brilliance? I am not that smart. No, it was research into what I believed at the time would be long-term trends. That decision years ago has permitted me to keep my business growing and my new sales acquisition costs to a minimum.

How did I do it? I read the books, articles, case studies—whatever I could get my hands on—by the futurists, and I still do it today. Who are these futurists? Here are a few of my favorites: Marvin Cetron, Roger Herman, Carolyn Corbin, John Naisbitt, William Strauss, Willis Harman, Paul Kennedy, Daniel Burris, Joe Pine, Jim Gilmore, and William Bridges.

If you want to guarantee your future career or business success, then I recommend you read at least two or three such books a year.

Turn It Around
Research trends that can impact your customers.

MISTAKE #89: *Not Asking*

Once a customer has been sold, there is an excellent opportunity to develop the relationship into a real winning relationship. But you have to ask for it. What would you like to have from this new client or customer?

How about:

- Referrals
- A letter of testimony
- The right to use them as a reference
- Repeat business
- Third-party influence
- A strategic alliance

What else can you think of?

Loyal customers, if you have enough of them, are a very valuable asset that can springboard your career just as fast as unsatisfied customers, if you have enough of them, can cause your career to take a nose dive.

Learning to ask for what you want and deserve from your customers, due to your exceptional service, is not only professional and acceptable, but is often expected by your customers. In fact, not asking a customer for any of the above can send a negative signal that you don't care, don't trust them or respect them, or don't feel they can help you.

Turn It Around
Learn to ask for what you deserve because of your service.

MISTAKE #90: *Going Only for the Home Runs*

Every now and then, salespeople hit a home run: they close a big deal. When this happens, you have the right to celebrate and pat yourself on the back for your patience, persistence, skill, and perseverance. Most salespeople, from time to time, no matter what they sell, have the opportunity or potential for a Big One. If you closed only these big sales from time to time and nothing else in between, you would most likely starve. Successful salespeople understand the concept of hitting singles and doubles while they are working on one of those biggies. Why? Because the big deals:

- Can take longer to close
- Generally require more work
- Can leave you with a big lost-sale hangover if they don't close
- Require more corporate resources
- Can take time away from the routine activities of closing the smaller deals
- Require a higher level of skill due to the nature of your contact

The critical factor is maintaining balance in the mix of big deals and smaller ones you are working on. Yes, a $100,000 deal could represent 20 percent of your quota for the year, but it could also take 50 percent of your time. Five $20,000 deals will tend to close faster and get you to the same outcome. What is in your pipeline? A lot of big deals? A few big deals? Just smaller ones? Again, the key is in the mix. The formula I use is ten to one: ten smaller active prospects in my pipeline to every big prospect.

The secret is to get the sales closed and then cultivate the client for more business. I would much rather have a higher repeat-business ratio than a higher new-sale close ratio. This strategy is not meant to give you permission to not focus on generating new customers. You can't upgrade a current customer until you have sold them the first time.

Turn It Around
Establish the right mix of prospects in your pipeline.

MISTAKE #91: *Not Seeing Current Customers as Prospects*

Many salespeople treat customers or clients as one-time sales opportunities. When they have this limited view, they fail to achieve additional sales opportunities with these customers. Not only is a client a client, but a client is always a prospect for something more.

In order to gain these kinds of results, the salesperson must have a repeat-business mentality. One of my favorite sales concepts is: make a sale and you'll make an income; sell a relationship and you'll make a fortune. Some of you may be thinking: *Tim, I am getting 100 percent of my client's business now; how can they be a prospect for more business?* There is more than one way to get more business from clients. They can also be a source of additional business by:

- giving you referrals
- letting you use them as a reference
- networking for you
- hiving you third-party influence
- introducing you to their friends or business associates

As you can see from the above list, there are many ways a client can help you get additional business—even if you already have 100 percent of their business, which is often unlikely. Don't underestimate the power of third-party influence to help you sell more in less time, with less energy, and less corporate resources. If your current customer is a resource for you, they can have a dramatic impact on your future sales success.

Remember, it is easier, less stressful, less time-consuming, and often more fun to do more business with a present customer than it is to keep finding more new customers.

Turn It Around
Use your customers to help increase your contacts and sales.

SALES QUIZ ANSWERS

Keep in mind that the answers to several of the questions are subjective. In many cases, there is no right or wrong answer, only a best or better answer. This quiz is not designed to give you an in-depth explanation for each answer, but rather to stimulate your thinking. With this in mind, let's take a look at what—after over forty years of selling and teaching people to sell worldwide—I believe some of the best answers are.

1. They talk too much. They give information before they get it.
2. It impacts every aspect of the sales process and sales relationship.
3. Characteristics or traits of a product or service.
4. What the features do for the customer.

5. The beginning of the customer relationship.
6. Positive, necessary sales signals.
7. Reading people, listening, and asking good questions.
8. The fear of rejection.
9. Ranking:
    1. Attitude management
    2. People skills
    3. Prospect qualifying
    4. Sales skills
    5. Presentation skills
    6. Product knowledge
    7. Closing techniques
10. They want, need, like, desire, can afford, or will benefit from the product or service.
11. emotionally; logically
12. You need to tell them to sell them.
13. Ranking:
    1. Service
    2. Quality
    3. Convenience
    4. Good terms
    5. Product/service reliability

6. Organization reputation

7. Price

14. From a sales attitude standpoint: at the beginning of the sales process. From a skill or strategic standpoint: when the prospect is ready to buy.

15. Being sold to.

16. Your current customer base, past customers, and referrals.

17. They give you credibility and reduce buyer fears and mistrust.

18. You can, but not well and not for long.

19. All the time.

20. It depends on how badly the customer perceives his need. Many times poor salespeople are able, with the help of good prospects, to make up for poor sales ability.

21. The one that is the most consistent with your own values or beliefs.

22. False.

23. False.

24. True.

25. False.

26. False.

27. Getting accurate information early in the sales process.
28. False.
29. False.
30. True.
31. True and False. It depends on a number of factors.
32. False.
33. False.
34. False.
35. False.
36. False.
37. It depends on a number of factors.
38. Trust.
39. They help you see where improvement will be helpful or necessary to achieve greater sales success.
40. Can I trust you and believe you? Are you looking out for my best interests or your own?
41. Being a better ongoing resource for your customers.
42. False.
43. It helps you spend time with only the best prospects.

44. It depends.
45. The prospect's office.
46. False.
47. Raise the perceived value.
48. True.
49. The ability to ask well-thought-out, timely, and intelligent questions, and then listen.
50. True.

Scoring:

50 correct answers	You should be giving the quiz.
45–49 correct answers	You are a real sales professional.
40–44 correct answers	There is hope for you yet.
35–39 correct answers	With luck, you may make it.
30–34 correct answers	You are losing a lot of business.
29 or less correct answers	You need help big-time—call me.

PERSONAL SKILL AND ATTITUDE ASSESSMENT

If you haven't already done so, now would be a good time to do a little self-evaluation on where you could use some improvements in your skills or attitudes. Under "Mistakes You Need to Turn Around," list those areas where you feel you could improve. Also rank each item's priority:

- Immediate (now)
- High (short term)
- Medium (next few months)
- Low (whenever you can get to it)

Make sure that as you prioritize these, you do it according to your need and not your comfort level.

Mistakes You Need to Turn Around

1. Attitudes

Priority:

Mistake:

Turn It Around:

Priority:

Mistake:

Turn It Around:

Priority:

Mistake:

Turn It Around:

Priority:

Mistake:

Turn It Around:

Priority:

Mistake:

Turn It Around:

Priority:

Mistake:

Turn It Around:

Priority:

Mistake:

Turn It Around:

Priority:

Mistake:

Turn It Around:

Priority:

Mistake:

Turn It Around:

Priority:

Mistake:

Turn It Around:

2. *Prospecting*

Priority:

Mistake:

Turn It Around:

Priority:

Mistake:

Turn It Around:

Priority:

Mistake:

Turn It Around:

Priority:

Mistake:

Turn It Around:

Priority:

Mistake:

Turn It Around:

Priority:

Mistake:

Turn It Around:

Priority:

Mistake:

Turn It Around:

Priority:

Mistake:

Turn It Around:

Priority:

Mistake:

Turn It Around:

Priority:

Mistake:

Turn It Around:

3. Sales Presentation

Priority:

Mistake:

Turn It Around:

Priority:

Mistake:

Turn It Around:

Priority:

Mistake:

Turn It Around:

Priority:

Mistake:

Turn It Around:

Priority:

Mistake:

Turn It Around:

Priority:

Mistake:

Turn It Around:

Priority:

Mistake:

Turn It Around:

Priority:

Mistake:

Turn It Around:

Priority:

Mistake:

Turn It Around:

Priority:

Mistake:

Turn It Around:

4. Handling Objections & Closing

Priority:

Mistake:

Turn It Around:

Priority:

Mistake:

Turn It Around:

Priority:

Mistake:

Turn It Around:

Priority:

Mistake:

Turn It Around:

Priority:

Mistake:

Turn It Around:

Priority:

Mistake:

Turn It Around:

Priority:

Mistake:

Turn It Around:

Priority:

Mistake:

Turn It Around:

Priority:

Mistake:

Turn It Around:

Priority:

Mistake:

Turn It Around:

5. *Time & Territory Management*

Priority:

Mistake:

Turn It Around:

Priority:

Mistake:

Turn It Around:

Priority:

Mistake:

Turn It Around:

Priority:

Mistake:

Turn It Around:

Priority:

Mistake:

Turn It Around:

Priority:

Mistake:

Turn It Around:

Priority:

Mistake:

Turn It Around:

6. *Record Keeping*

Priority:

Mistake:

Turn It Around:

Priority:

Mistake:

Turn It Around:

Priority:

Mistake:

Turn It Around:

Priority:

Mistake:

Turn It Around:

7. *After-Sales Service*

Priority:

Mistake:

Turn It Around:

Priority:

Mistake:

Turn It Around:

Priority:

Mistake:

Turn It Around:

Priority:

Mistake:

Turn It Around:

Priority:

Mistake:

Turn It Around:

Personal Skill and Attitude Action Plan

Okay, now that you know where some improvement is called for, it is time to move past the words and into the action. Knowing and not doing is the same as not knowing. Why not use a rating system here, too? It will help ensure that you follow through. Rank each item's priority:

- Immediate (now)
- High (short term)
- Medium (next few months)
- Low (whenever you can get to it)

Make sure that as you prioritize these, you do it according to your need and not your comfort level.

Action Areas for Development	Priority	Completion Date Goal

Action Areas for Development	Priority	Completion Date Goal

SUMMARY

Here are the fifteen biggest mistakes salespeople make:
1. They talk too much.
2. They give information before they get information.
3. They fail to observe and integrate early prospect signals.
4. They fail to effectively manage rejection and failure.
5. They sell when they should prospect, and prospect when they should sell.
6. They don't listen and take notes while the prospect is talking.
7. They inject their own values or buying prejudices into the sales process.

8. They don't effectively read buyer signals and act accordingly.

9. They sell features and price rather than value and customer benefits.

10. They don't keep good records or evaluate their wins and losses.

11. They don't work as hard to keep the business as they did to get it.

12. They don't ask for the business.

13. They focus on making the sale rather than selling the relationship.

14. They don't invest enough time and money in their self-development.

15. They confuse the importance of knowing with that of caring.

Now here are the traits of successful salespeople:

1. They manage their attitudes from inside-out instead of outside-in.
2. They are on fire with passion and desire.
3. They are a resource for their clients. They go the extra mile.
4. They are excellent communicators.
5. They are focused and concentrate on the task at hand.
6. They are able to win the support of all inside support staff.
7. They spend more time getting information than giving it.
8. They are masters at asking the right questions, in the right way, at the right time.
9. They sell value, not price. They know that, over time, this is the most important issue to the customer.
10. They manage their resources of time, corporate resources, money, and people.
11. They keep in touch with their clients on a regular basis.

12. Their primary goal is service and customer loyalty.
13. They honor their commitments.
14. They give something back to their community and their profession.
15. They are everywhere. They network and understand the value of good contacts.
16. They have lofty goals. They don't always reach them, but they aim for the stars.
17. They promise a lot and deliver more.
18. They understand the importance of knowledge of customers, competitors, and the marketplace.
19. Their word is their bond.
20. They work hard and smart.

Only in growth, reform, and change,
paradoxically enough, is true security
to be found.

—ANNE MORROW LINDBERGH

ARE SALESPEOPLE BECOMING OBSOLETE?

Will the continuous advances in technology replace the profession of selling in the foreseeable future? I am not a fortune teller or a mystic, but I do believe that we will see dramatic changes in the roles salespeople play in their organizations and the economy in general. During the next several years, and stretching into the next few decades, there will be dramatic and all-encompassing change in every industry, field, and profession. No one will go untouched by the swath that will cut across every age group and discipline.

We are rapidly becoming a society in which people no longer talk to each other face to face. We communicate by fax machine, computer, email, answering machines, and voice mail. We are losing the human touch. I believe there are a number of reasons why the sales profession is alive and well and will continue to be so for years.

Here are ten reasons why salespeople will play a vital role in a growing economy. Salespeople are charged with any or all of the following:

1. They present new ideas, concepts, products, and services to current clients and customers and to potential clients and customers alike.
2. They assess the marketplace, gauging customer satisfaction levels and perceptions, general market attitudes, competitor strengths and weaknesses, and consumer interest trends.
3. They witness and report on the emergence of grassroots market shifts and interests.
4. They soothe the ruffled egos of disappointed, frustrated, and angry customers.
5. They provide bottom-up feedback to the management of their organization on any number of opportunities, problems, and issues.
6. They are the front line of attack for any number of corporate marketing strategies and programs.

7. They work the trade show booths (a grueling task, if you have never done it) in thousands of trade shows each year.
8. They are on the look out for new product and service opportunities that a "corporate" person would never see.
9. They solve customer problems caused by poor design, poor production, poor distribution, and poor billing practices.
10. They are ambassadors for management, building positive on-going relationships that can increase business and profits.

I challenge you to find a computer, fax machine, software program, customer service rep, or marketing person who can do all of this with the courage of a mountain climber, the patience of Job, the sacrifice of Mother Teresa, the energy of a two-year-old, the creativity of Frank Lloyd Wright, the dedication of a mother, the wisdom of Confucius, the enthusiasm of a cheerleader, the commitment of an Olympic athlete, or the persistence of a toddler.

The role of the sales professional will continue to undergo transformation, but the fundamental mission will remain intact.

RECOMMENDED READING

James Allen, *As a Man Thinketh*

Tony Alessandra, *Non-Manipulative Selling*

Max Aitken Beaverbrook, *The Three Keys to Success*

William T. Brooks, *Niche Selling*

Bob Buford, *Halftime*

Russell Conwell, *Acres of Diamonds*

George S. Clason, *Richest Man in Babylon*

Tim Connor, *How to Sell More in Less Time*

Tim Connor, *Sales Mastery*

Tim Connor, *Soft Sell*

Tim Connor, *The Ancient Scrolls*

Tim Connor, *Win-Win Selling*

George W. Dudley, *Earning What You Are Worth*

William Exton, *Sales Leverage*

Stephen E. Heiman and Robert B. Miller, *Conceptual Selling*

Napoleon Hill, *Think and Grow Rich*

Lou Holtz, *Winning Every Day*

Kerry L. Johnson, *Sales Magic*

Charles E. Jones, *Life Is Tremendous*

Jim Meisenheimer, *47 Ways to Sell Smarter*

Jim Meisenheimer, *50 More Ways to Sell Smarter*

Arthur Mortell, *Anatomy of a Successful Salesman*

Og Mandino, *The Greatest Salesman in the World*

Og Mandino, *The Greatest Secret in the World*

William M. Marston, *Emotions of Normal People*

Norman Vincent Peale, *The Power of Positive Thinking*

Al Ries and Jack Trout, *The 22 Immutable Laws of Marketing*

Art Sobczak, *Telephone Tips that Sell*

Hank Trisler, *No Bull Selling*

Thomas J. Winninger, *Price Wars*

INDEX

A

Adversity
  learning, 21
  reaction, 80
After-sales problems, solution, 11
After-sales service
  impact, 72. See also Customers
  issues, handling, 206
  laws, 231, 234–239
  mistakes, 231–239
    index, 17–18
    turn-around, 265–266
  turn-arounds, index, 25
Alter ego, attempt
  mistake, 14, 62–63
  turn-around, 63
Asking
  absence
    mistake, 18, 244–245
    turn-around, 245
  importance, 22
Attitude
  control, 72
  daily improvement, 25
  importance, 3
  management, 4
  mistakes, 27–28
    index, 13–14
    turn-around, 258–259
  turn-arounds, index, 19–21

B

Balance, absence
  countering steps, 69
  mistake, 14, 68–69
  turn-around, 69
Begging, unattractiveness, 124
Benchmarks
  consideration, 227

establishment, absence
  mistake, 17, 226–228
  turn-around, 228
Big Pow Wow, 146
Business
  asking, 72
  asking, absence
    mistake, 16, 186–187
    turn-around, 187
  regaining, 107
  repetition, 244
  resource, 22
  sources, 6
Business loss
  nonfight
    mistake, 15, 110–111
    turn-around, 111
  strategy, 21
Business need, acting
  mistake, 15, 124–125
  turn-around, 125
Buying urgency, creation, 21

C

Call-back approach, precision
  (absence)
    mistake, 15, 136–137
    turn-around, 137
Career
  advocates, development, 210
  passion, liveliness, 19
  strategic alliances, development, 211
  success, 20
  ups/downs, recognition, 20
Chastity (virtue), 88
Cleanliness (virtue), 87–88
Clear focus, absence
  mistake, 13, 30–31

turn-around, 31
Clear goals, absence
  mistake, 14, 74–75
  turn-around, 75
Clear purpose, absence
  mistake, 13, 36–37
  turn-around, 37
Closing
  methodology, 24
  mistakes
    handling, 173–177
    index, 16–17
    turn-around, 262–263
  strategy, absence
    mistake, 16, 188–191
    turn-around, 191
  success, reasons, 191
  techniques, 4
  turn-arounds, index, 23–24
Cold calling, effectiveness, 8
Comfort zone, remaining
  mistake, 15, 108–109
  turn-around, 109
Commitments
  honoring, 20, 35, 238
  questions, 65
Competitors
  ignoring
    mistake, 15, 132–133
    turn-around, 133
  knowledge, 22, 210
Compliment, reaction, 53
Concentration, importance, 34
Concessions
  addressing, 24
  advertising
    mistake, 16, 192–193
    turn-around, 193
Contacts (increase), customers
  (usage), 25
Control, planned approach (usage),
  22
Corporate attitude, law, 235–236
Customer benefits
  focus, 22
  selling, absence
    mistake, 16, 156–157
    turn-around, 157

Customers
  appreciation, 238
  concern, law, 235
  contact, 21
    maintenance, 206
  incorrectness, law, 234–235
  loss, reasons, 106
  loyalty (increase), after-sales serv-
    ice (impact), 7
  problem-solving attitude, usage,
    239
  progress, informing, 238
  prospect perspective, absence
    mistake, 18, 248–249
    turn-around, 249
  referral request, 22
    timing, 6
  relationships, cultivation, 206
  service, 11
    length, 235–236
  time, availability, 236–237
  training, input, 235–236

D

Daily improvement, failure
  mistake, 17, 229–230
  turn-around, 230
Daily self-improvement, 20
Decision maker
  presentations, giving, 22
Decision makers
  noncontact
    mistake, 15, 130–131
    turn-around, 131
Defining statement
  conciseness, absence
    mistake, 16, 152–153
    turn-around, 153
  ingredients, 152–153
Delivery terms, 199
Discouragement
  mistake, 14, 58–59
  turn-around, 59
Discipline, price, 20, 60
Disorganization
  mistake, 13, 34–35
  turn-around, 35

E

Effectiveness, increase, 66
Ego. See Alter ego
  blockage
    mistake, 14, 76–77
    turn-around, 77
Elevator questions
  development, 22
  forgetting
    mistake, 15, 128–129
    turn-around, 129
Emotional/psychological anchors,
  development, 210
Employees, customer status, 237
Excitement, loss
  mistake, 13, 38–39
  turn-around, 39
Expectations management, absence
  mistake, 14, 84–85
  turn-around, 85

F

Failure
  impossibility, 19
  negative perspective
    mistake, 13, 44–45
    turn-around, 45
  overcoming, 80
  reaction, 52
  success, relationship, 19
Feature-based presentation, problems, 157
Features, 199
  selling
    mistake, 16, 156–157
    turn-around, 157
Financial terms, 199
Focus. See Clear focus
  importance, 19
  loss
    mistake, 17, 208–209
    turn-around, 209
Follow-up process, absence
  mistake, 17, 240–241
  turn-around, 241
Follow-up sales call, considerations,
  137

Follow-up strategy
  absence, 114
  development, 21
  usage, 22
Frugality (virtue), 87
Future living. See Past/future living
Futurists, 243

G

Gatekeeper, challenge, 11
Goals. See Clear goals
  achievement, 66
  prioritization, 34
Goal-setting activities, routine time,
  20
Gratitude
  absence
    mistake, 13, 48–49
    turn-around, 49
  display, 20
Growth/change, terms, 20

H

High value, selling (absence)
  mistake, 16, 154–155
  turn-around, 155
Home runs (big deals), sole attempts
  mistake, 18, 246–247
  turn-around, 247
Human touch, technology (interfer-
  ence), 24
Humility (virtue), 88

I

Identification, 140
Illusions, release, 21
Improvement. See Daily improve-
  ment; Daily self-improvement
Income, improvement, 66
Industry (virtue), 87
Information, sending (question)
  mistake, 15, 114–115
  turn-around, 115
Inside-out living, 20
Integrity, absence
  mistake, 13, 56–57
  turn-around, 57

Intent, honesty (absence)
  mistake, 14, 64–65
  turn-around, 65
Internet, sales ease, 8

J

Journal
  helpfulness, 66
  initiation/continuation, 20
Justice (virtue), 87

L

Learning stoppage
  mistake, 13, 32–33
  turn-around, 33
Life
  balance, 20
  gratefulness, 48–49
  importance, decision, 19
  passion, liveliness, 19
  problem, reaction, 52
Life slippage
  mistake, 14, 66–67
  turn-around, 67
Lifestyle, improvement, 66
Listening, absence
  mistake, 16, 166–167
  reasons, 166
  turn-around, 167
Lost-sale strategy, absence
  mistake, 16, 194–195
  turn-around, 195
Low price, selling
  mistake, 16, 154–155
  turn-around, 155

M

Memories, capture, 66
Mentors
  definition, 46
  usage, 19
Mind/energy, usage, 19
Mistakes, 3
  index, 13–18
  introduction, 1–2
  learning/wisdom, 21
  summary, 269–272
  turn-around, 258–266

Mistakes repetition
  mistake, 14, 86–88
  turn-around, 88
Moderation (virtue), 87

N

Negotiation, 10
  selling, contrast
    mistake, 17, 198–199
    turn-around, 199
  timing, understanding, 24
Networking, infrequency
  mistake, 15, 112–113
  turn-around, 113
No sale result, 188
Numbers selling
  mistake, 14, 98–99
  turn-around, 99

O

Objections
  answering, techniques, 23
  early disarmament, absence
    mistake, 16, 178–179
    turn-around, 179
  mistakes
    handling, 173–177
    index, 16–17
    turn-around, 262–263
  turn-arounds, index, 23–24
Objectives, prioritization, 34
Obstacles, overcoming, 80
Optimism, 20
  reality/forecasting, combination,
    24
Order
  asking, 24
  request, timing, 7
Order, virtue, 87
Organization, reputation, 5
Outside-in living
  mistake, 14, 82–83
  turn-around, 83

P

Passion, enthusiasm (contrast), 38
Past clients, ignoring
  mistake, 15, 106–107

turn-around, 107
Past/future living
    mistake, 14, 91
    turn-around, 91
Patience
    absence
        mistake, 14, 70–71
        turn-around, 71
    perspectives, 70
People
    change, 104–105, 126
    dislikes, 6
    emotional/logical purchases/deci-
        sions, 5
    invalidation, tendency, 164
    skills, 4
    types, 54
People, purchases, 9
    mistake, 15, 104–105
    reasons, 5
    turn-around, 105
Personal biases, projection
    mistake, 16, 184–185
    turn-around, 185
Personal coach, usage, 19
Personal issues, career roles (separa-
    tion), 208–209
Personal management, approach
    method, 34–35
Personal sales call, telephone sales
    call (contrast), 7
Personal skill/attitude action plan,
    266–268
Personal skill/attitude assessment,
    257–268
Pessimism
    mistake, 13, 50–51
    turn-around, 51
Planning/finishing, completion, 19
Poor prospects, time management
    mistake, 17, 216–217
    turn-around, 217
Present (time), focus, 21
Presentations. See Decision makers;
    Sales presentations; Tailored pre-
    sentations
    skills, 4

tailoring, 22
Price objections
    problem perspective
        mistake, 16, 180–181
        turn-around, 181
    rejection, 23
Privacy, importance, 238–239
Problems
    negative perspective
        mistake, 14, 89–90
        turn-around, 90
    ownership, law, 236
Product
    customer benefits, 3
    features, 3
    knowledge, 4
    level, energy/time (devotion), 100
    reliability, 5
    self-selling, 7
Projects, prioritization, 34
Promises, keeping, 20, 238
Prospect profile
    nonusage
        mistake, 15, 140–141
        turn-around, 141
    usage, 24
Prospecting
    approaches, attempts, 21
    effectiveness, 72
    elements, 140
    mistakes, 93–96
        index, 14–15
        turn-around, 259–260
    turn-arounds, index, 21–22
Prospects
    concerns, 5
        importance, 10
    contact, 206
    emotional buying motive, learn-
        ing, 23
    invalidation
        mistake, 16, 164–165
        turn-around, 165
    loss, understanding, 24
    mix, establishment, 25
    practice
        mistake, 15, 118–119

turn-around, 119
price challenge, 11
profile, effectiveness, 10
qualification, 4
   systematic method, usage, 22
quality, importance, 21
questions, asking, 119
referral request, 22
relating, absence
   mistake, 16, 160–161
   turn-around, 161
respect/concern, 23
segments, 104
selling time, 8
talking, quantity, 22
understanding, 23
visitation, 9
words, understanding, 23
Psychological debt
building, failure
   mistake, 15, 134–135
   turn-around, 135
creation, service (usage), 22
Purpose. See Clear purpose
motivator, 36

Q
Qualification, 140
Quitting
   mistake, 13, 40–41
   reasons, 40
   turn-around, 41

R
Reading, recommendations, 277–278
Record keeping
absence
   mistake, 17, 222–223
   turn-around, 223
guidelines, creation, 25
mistakes, 219–221
   index, 17
   turn-around, 264–265
turn-arounds, index, 25
References, value, 6
Referrals, 244
Referrals, question (forgetting)

mistake, 15, 138–139
   turn-around, 139
Regret, price, 20
Rejection, reaction, 80
Rejection fear
   mistake, 15, 116–117
   reaction, 117
   turn-around, 117
Relationship
   competition proofing, 10
   improvement, 66
   level, energy/time (devotion), 101
Relaxation, importance, 20
Resolution (virtue), 87
Resource, becoming (absence)
   mistake, 15, 142–143
   turn-around, 143
Results, evaluation, 25
absence
   mistake, 17, 224–225
   turn-around, 225
Risks, taking, 80

S
Sales
   call, follow-up, 115
   close, 4, 8
     focus, 94
     increase, 10
     initiation, 6
   cycles, control, 21
   facts, writing, 25
   failure, cause, 4
   forecasting, quality (absence)
     mistake, 17, 212–213
     turn-around, 213
   increase, customers (usage), 25
   loss
     reactions, 110, 194–195
     saving, 24
   message
     customization, 23
     planning, 11
   obtaining, prospect (input), 5
   ongoing relationship, connection,
     23
   quiz, 3–12

answers, 251–256
records, importance, 10
resistance, early discovery, 23
rituals, development, 210
skills, 4
    importance, 4
slumps, impact
    mistake, 14, 72–73
    turn-around, 73
success, ranking, 4
time, usage/planning, 24
timing, understanding, 24
transaction perspective
    mistake, 16, 162–163
    turn-around, 163
Sales cycle victim
    mistake, 15, 102–103
    turn-around, 103
Sales objections, 4
    fear
        mistake, 16, 182–183
        turn-around, 183
Sales presentations, 150–151
    mistakes, 144–148
        index, 16
        turn-around, 261–262
    small talk, importance, 11
    turn-arounds, index, 22–23
Sales process
    control, loss
        mistake, 15, 122–123
        turn-around, 123
    ego, absence, 20
    importance, 8
    neutrality, 23
Salespeople
    follow-up, absence (reasons), 136
    obsolescence, 273–276
    techniques, practice, 22
Self-appreciation, increase, 20
Self-belief, 20
    absence
        mistake, 13, 54–55
        turn-around, 55
Self-confidence
    absence

mistake, 14, 80–81
    turn-around, 81
    reaction, 81
Self-development program, 33
Self-discipline, absence
    mistake, 14, 60–61
    turn-around, 61
Self-esteem, nonimprovement
    mistake, 13, 52–53
    turn-around, 53
Self-help material, reading, 210
Self-imposed limitations
    mistake, 13, 42–43
    turn-around, 43
Self-improvement, investment, 18
Self-investment, 32
Selling. See Numbers selling
    competitiveness, 229
    event/process, contrast, 7
    homogeneity
        mistake, 16, 158–159
        turn-around, 159
    readiness
        mistake, 17, 210–211
        turn-around, 211
    requirements, 198–199
    skills, 12
    timing, understanding, 24
    wrong level
        mistake, 14, 100–101
        turn-around, 101
Service level, energy/time (devotion),
    100
Service reliability, 5
Shared fate level, energy/time (devo-
    tion), 101
Silence (virtue), 87
Sincerity (virtue), 87
Skills, daily improvement, 25
Solution level, energy/time (devo-
    tion), 100–101
Stakeholder level, energy/time (devo-
    tion), 101
Strategic alliance, 244
Stress
    management, absence

mistake, 14, 78–79
  turn-around, 79
  reaction, self-decision, 20
Success, reaction, 53
Surrender, impossibility, 19

T

Tailored presentations
  ignoring
      mistake, 16, 150–151
      turn-around, 151
  impact, 72
Talking, excess
  mistake, 15, 120–121
  turn-around, 121
Tasks
  prioritization, 34
  routines, importance, 34
Technology
  change, 105
  crutch
      mistake, 17, 206–207
      turn-around, 207
  tool, usage, 35
  user-friendliness, 237
Temperance (virtue), 87
Territory, business source, 24
Territory management
  mistakes, 201–203
      index, 17
      turn-around, 263–264
  quality, absence
      mistake, 17, 214–215
      turn-around, 215
  turn-arounds, index, 24
Testimonials, value, 6
Third-party influence, 244
Time
  respect/value, 35
  saving, 66
Time management
  mistakes, 201–203
      index, 17
      turn-around, 263–264
  turn-arounds, index, 24
  usage
      mistake, 17, 204–205

  turn-around, 205
Total achievement, self-attempt
  mistake, 13, 46–47
  turn-around, 47
Tranquility (virtue), 88
Transaction level, energy/time (devotion), 100
Trend watching, absence
  mistake, 18, 242–243
  turn-around, 243
Trends
  research, 25
  types, 242
Trust
  building, earliness
      mistake, 15, 126–127
      turn-around, 127
  building, focus, 21
  establishment, 22
      focus, 21
Truth, usage, 20
Turn-arounds, index, 19–25

U

Up-selling, 119
Urgency. See Buying urgency
  sense, creation (failure)
      mistake, 16, 170–171
      turn-around, 171

V

Value, perception (creation), 23
Verbal messages, non-verbal messages (accuracy contrast), 8
Virtues, 87–88
Vocabulary, inadequacy
  mistake, 16, 168–169
  turn-around, 169
Voice mail, challenge, 11

W

Walk-away power, absence
  mistake, 17, 196–197
  turn-around, 197
Words, power (knowledge), 23
Workspace, organization, 35

ABOUT THE AUTHOR

Tim Connor, CSP, is the president and CEO of Connor Resource Group Inc. and Peak Performance Institute. He has been a full-time professional speaker, trainer, coach, consultant, and bestselling author for thirty-three years. Since 1973, he has given over four thousand presentations in twenty-one countries around the world to a wide variety of audiences.

Each year over 85 percent of his presentations are return engagements for previous clients on such topics as peak performance management, effective leadership, customer-focused sales strategies, personal motivation, value-driven customer service, and building positive business and personal relationships.

Each year he also facilitates a number of strategic planning events and meetings for many of his clients and presents several public boot camps. He is a results-oriented business coach and consultant working with a select few clients each year to help them improve their individual and organizational performance.

Tim has been a member of the National Speakers Association for over twenty-five years, and he is one of only four hundred Certified Speaking Professionals in the world, a designation bestowed by the National Speakers Association since 1980.

He is the bestselling author of fifty-seven books, including the international bestsellers *Soft Sell*, *The Ancient Scrolls*, and *Your First Year in Sales*.

Tim's clients range from companies with five million a year in sales to those with over fifty billion in sales, and come from a wide variety of industries, including food manufacturing and distribution, housing and construction, financial services, technology and communication, manufacturing, and personal and professional services.

His presentations are filled with insightful and contemporary ideas and are presented in a riveting and entertaining style.

To discuss hiring Tim for your organization,
contact him at:
Phone: 704-895-1230
Fax: 704-895-1231
Email: tim@timconnor.com
Website: www.timconnor.com